WOMEN'S GODDESS RETREAT
FACILITATOR'S
HANDBOOK

LAURELEI BLACK

Women's Goddess Retreat — Facilitator's Handbook
By Laurelei Black
Cover Design by Laurelei Black

ISBN-13: 978-1-956765-30-4 (paperback)
ISBN-13: 978-1-956765-29-8 (digital book)

We are a CIRCLE

Within a CIRCLE

With no beginning

... and never ending!

For all the women of the retreat.

For Holly, Honey, Gwenhwyvar, Sharon, Amanda, Shay, Fern, Sharon, Shannon, and Hillary — who have helped facilitate the Midian retreat year after tireless year.

For Natalie — who conceived of this magic and tossed the first pebble into the pond.

Table of Contents

Message from Laurelei

Greetings, Goddess Friends!

I am beginning the undertaking of this handbook just three short weeks before our 2024 retreat begins, and I am motivated by a desire to do everything in my power to ensure the continuity of our important work long after my own ability to facilitate it has ended.

I think we might already be there, in some ways. We've had a culture of transparency, shared leadership, and delegation since our first retreat, back in 2009. And in the intervening years, many of you have stepped up to lead circles, take on behind-the-scenes tasks, and even lead and facilitate similar retreats closer to your own homes.

This book is addressed to you. My Sisters, Mothers, Daughters, and Friends. At the time I'm writing this, I assume that I know your face and name, and that you know mine. I'm assuming that we've sat in circle together. Cried. Laughed. Screamed. Eaten. Danced. All together. If that hasn't been our literal experience — if this book has found its way to you in the mysterious ways that books and ideas so often do — then you are also my Sister, Mother, Daughter, Friend; and this book is as much for you as it is for the ones whose hair I've brushed, hands I've held, tears I've honored, and smiles I've celebrated.

What might you do with this book? Marvelous things, I hope! Those things might include:

- Helping to facilitate the original annual retreat

- Hosting a similar retreat at another location

- Reflecting on experiences you've had at past retreats

- Integrating the principles of this retreat into your daily life

- Creating an entirely new event or experience for a different group of people

Thank you for all the ways you are part of this community and this work. It has been one of the greatest privileges of my life to share space with this retreat community. I have been forever changed by your wisdom, grace, support, and experience.

Message from Natalie

The first Women's Goddess Retreat came to me in a vision of the Goddess Hera. I had been feeling frustrated over group dynamics at the festival grounds I used to frequent and was meditating on a solution. I had recently read The Millionth Circle and The Women's Retreat Book, and I was contemplating how circles of women can create and strengthen community, but was struggling with how to put those ideas into practice.

Hera appeared radiant and regal, demanding that I create a circle of, by, and for women in her honor. Based on this vision, I began forming an outline of what the Women's Goddess Retreat would become.

The first retreat consisted of 13 Goddesses, chosen from cultures throughout time, and around the world. Hera was, of course, among the original 13, but was not the focus. For that focus, my then wife Laurelei and I wanted to feature a way for women to understand that they themselves embodied the Goddess in an experiential way. This became the circle of The Great Goddess.

The first Women's Goddess Retreat was beautiful and imperfect in delightful ways. We were plagued with a few too many guided meditations, and a little too much "I can do it all myself" spirit, but we learned to share the circles with our sisters in the coming years.

What I did not expect to happen was to watch this community of women develop their own rites of passage, from birth through death. Truly, Hera's blessing had built something powerful that reshaped our lives.

Purpose of the Women's Goddess Retreat

When Natalie Long first envisioned this retreat in the spring and summer of 2008, she created a website that beautifully expressed the reasons why this retreat was formed. I've included almost all of her original language into various parts of this book (credited, of course) so that we might all remember our roots as we continue to spread our wings.

To address **WHY WE GATHER**, Natalie wrote:

At its core, our retreat intends to:

Provide a safe, nurturing place for women to develop themselves individually and as a group through new skills and the sharing of information,

And

Learn about, invoke, and honor Goddesses and Goddess spirituality from a variety of pantheons and cultures.

This retreat is designed to honor different Goddesses from various world cultures each year. Throughout the course of the retreat, each of the selected Goddesses for this year will be invoked by all participants for two hours each. During that time, we will share stories of that Goddess, perform group activities in honor of Her, and look to her stories and our inner wisdom for Her lessons in our own lives. At the end of each two hour session, we will release that Goddess's energy and have time for quiet reflection.

Retreats can deal with difficult subjects, and can be challenging to the participants. If you have attended outdoor festivals before, you will find this retreat will be different from past events. Retreat participants are encouraged to be present at all retreat events from Friday to Sunday, not including campsite set-up and tear-down.

During the retreat, you may be tempted to skip some of the scheduled group events. Ask yourself sincerely what you need at that moment, and then take whatever time you need to rest, reflect, and reconnect with yourself. Your journey is your own personal private path to renewal and you know what your spirit needs most. We ask only that you trust in the alchemical magic and process of the retreat, which is both challenging and rewarding.

Why a Women's Retreat?

Because women tend to nurture relationships more than they nurture themselves, it is often a challenge for women to carve out the space and time they need for private renewal and reflection. We believe that women feel and hear the gentle call to retreat and reflect as the voice of the Goddess. At the Women's Goddess Retreat we come together as sisters, mothers, daughters, lovers, friends, and women to celebrate this call, to honor her place within us and our place within the world.

> "All women go through periods in their lives when numerous demands are placed on them —family, work, spouse, ex-spouse, children, stepchildren, parents. It is important, indeed necessary, to step back and re-evaluate one's priorities, to reflect on one's mission in life. For it is only in nurturing one's soul that one can nurture, take care of another. Sometimes, one must say, "Stop! Listen to me. I have a story to tell."

~ Mary Michalia,© Chicken Soup For The Woman's Soul

Who Is This Retreat For?

The Women's Goddess Retreat was created for all women who want to pause and honor the Goddess in their lives and in themselves. This retreat is open to anyone who lives their daily life as a woman. Both women-born-women and transgender women are welcome at this retreat.

This retreat is open to our daughters at the discretion of their mothers. We recommend young women be at the age of menarche and are deemed by their mother to be mature enough to handle themes of women's sexuality, trauma, healing, and aging. Special rates are available to young women age 18 and under.

In honor of our beloved elders a special discounted admission rate is available to all women age 60 and older.

What is a Retreat?

A retreat is the act of temporarily removing oneself from one's usual environment in order to become immersed in a particular subject matter. A retreat can be taken for reasons related to spirituality, stress, health, lifestyle, or social concerns.

A retreat can either be a time of solitude or a community experience. Some retreats are held in silence, while at others there may be a great deal of conversation, depending on the facilitators and the participants. Retreats are often conducted at rural or remote locations, either privately, or at a retreat center.

A retreat serves the body, mind and spirit by allowing time to find greater inner peace. When you find inner peace, you move the world toward peace. This is why it is vital to escape from the world's bombardment of sounds and images and take time for the mind and heart to come to stillness.

Retreat practice provides the opportunity for you to restore your energies, have time to rest and to let go of the day to day mundane responsibilities and focus on your own inner development and spiritual growth. You can learn to nurture yourself, restore a sense of balance and well-being, and open up to nature. A weight may seem to be lifted from your shoulders and you may be able to experience a fresh perspective that will renew your appreciation for life and your commitment to appreciate and use every precious moment.

Spiritual Retreats

Spiritual retreats like the Women's Goddess Retreat focus on the following:

- Discovery: Spiritual retreats allow you to discover a whole new self and help you in removing the limitations that your mind is occupied with. These retreats also allow you to discover a whole new perspective towards life.

- Transformation: Spiritual healing retreats allow you to transform your perspective and focus on things besides your daily life and work; these retreats help you find new paths in life.

- Participation: These spiritual retreats usually have group activities. Participating in these activities helps in increasing your confidence level.

- Intention: Retreats are arranged with an intent in mind. Our statement of intent is here. You may also want to consider your own personal intentions for going on retreat.

Choosing a Personal Intention

People go on retreat for a number of reasons that generally focus on positive personal change. You may be seeking a retreat for a number of reasons. Ask yourself if on this retreat you would like to:

- Relax at a deep level
- Rejuvenate your Spirit
- Take time for reflection
- Gain clarity on an issue or your life path
- Find meaning in your life beyond daily or material concerns
- Heal
- Practice your Faith
- Contemplate
- Create
- Women's Retreat

Retreat Literature

There are many great books about taking a retreat of your own, or for taking on retreat with you. Here are some of our favorites.

Books to Inspire a Women's Retreat

Woman's Retreat Book: A Guide to Restoring, Rediscovering and Reawakening Your True Self --In a Moment, An Hour, Or a Weekend - Jennifer Louden

This is our favorite retreat book and one we return to again and again! This book is perfect for creating your own retreat time and inspired the Women's Goddess Retreat.

The Millionth Circle: How to Change Ourselves and The World--The Essential Guide to Women's Circles— Jean Shinoda Bolen

This slim and powerful book is written like poetry and speaks of a vision to change the world one circle of women at a time.

Succulent Wild Woman—SARK

All of SARK's books are full of juicy life and succulent inspiration. This is her opus, and our retreat's manifesto!

Imagine a Woman in Love with Herself: Embracing Your Wisdom and Wholeness—Patricia Lynn Reilly (Excerpt. © All rights reserved.)

> Imagine a woman who believes it is right and good she is a woman.
>
> A woman who honors her experience and tells her stories.
>
> Who refuses to carry the sins of others within her body and life.
>
> Imagine a woman who has acknowledged the past's influence on the present.
>
> A woman who has walked through her past.
>
> Who has healed into the present.

Imagine a woman who names her own gods.

A woman who imagines the divine in her image and likeness.

Who designs her own spirituality and allows it to inform her daily life.

Imagine a woman in love with her own body.

A woman who believes her body is enough, just as it is.

Who celebrates her body's rhythms and cycles as an exquisite resource.

Imagine a woman who honors the body of the Goddess in her changing body.

A woman who celebrates the accumulation of her years and her wisdom.

Who refuses to use her precious life-energy disguising the changes in her body and life.

Imagine a woman who values the women in her life.

A woman who sits in circles of women.

Who is reminded of the truth about herself when she forgets.

IMAGINE YOURSELF AS THIS WOMAN.

Women Who Run with the Wolves—Clarissa Pinkola Estes

This book contains enough deep inner working material for a lifetime of retreats. It explores the development of a woman's soul through story and her wild nature. One of our favorites.

Circle of Stones: Woman's Journey to Herself—Judith Duerk

A book of women's self reflection, unfolding, and spirituality.

Gift from the Sea—Anne Morrow Lindbergh

A classic reflection of one woman's time retreating by the sea. Timeless, and full of meaning.

The Heroine's Journey—Maureen Murdock

Explores how women can carve out their own journey to self realization and wholeness through archetypical symbolism and mythology.

Natalie also created, in those early days, a very nice booklist that can be seen on the following two pages of this book. This list is currently available through the WGR webpage maintained at AsteriaBooks.com.

These have remained our core reasons for gathering — to honor the Goddesses of the world, and to better understand and honor our own Divine Selves through their stories and our own.

Womens Goddess Retreat Book List

There are many great books about taking a retreat of your own, or for taking on retreat with you. Here are some of our favorites. They have been grouped into categories but many of them belong in more than one section.

Books About Women's Retreats and Circles
A Retreat of My Own by Karen Ely
A Weekend to Change Your Life by Joan Anderson
Breathing Space: Mini-retreats for the Heart and Soul by Karen Ely
Circle of Stones by Judith Duerk
I Sit Listening to the Wind by Judith Duerk
The Woman's Retreat Book by Jennifer Louden
20-Minute Retreats by Dr. Rachel Harris
Sacred Circles by Robin Deen Carnes & Sally Craig
Calling the Circle by Christina Baldwin
The Millionth Circle by Jean Shinoda Bolen
Girl Group Confidential by Jennifer Worick

Books to Take on a Women's Retreat for Inspiration
A Year by the Sea: Thoughts of an Unfinished Woman by Joan Anderson
Becoming Fully Human by Joan Chittister
Broken Open: How Difficult Times Can Help Us Grow by Elizabeth Lesser
Daring to Dream: Reflections on the Year I Found Myself by Karen Ely
Deep Water Passage by Ann Linnea
Drinking the Rain by Alix Kates Shulman
Eat, Pray, Love by Elizabeth Gilbert
Floor Sample by Julia Cameron
Gift from the Sea by Anne Morrow Lindbergh
I Will Not Die an Unlived Life by Dawna Markova
I Know Why the Caged Bird Sings by Maya Angelou
Imagine a Woman in Love with Herself by Patricia Lynn Reilly
Journal of a Solitude by May Sarton
Kitchen Table Wisdom by Rachel Naomi Remen
Let's Take the Long Way Home: A Memoir of Friendship by Gail Caldwell
Long, Quiet Highway by Natalie Goldberg
Mountains Beyond Mountains by Tracy Kidder
My Grandfather's Blessings by Rachel Naomi Remen
Out of Africa by Isak Dinesen
Pilgrim at Tinker Creek by Annie Dillard
Refuge by Terry Tempest Williams
Seasons of Change by Carol L. McClelland
Spot of Grace by Dawna Markova
Succulent Wild Woman by SARK
The Circle Of Life by Joyce Rupp & Macrina Wiederkehr
The Color Purple by Alice Walker
The Road from Coorain by Jill Ker Conway
The Woman at Otowi Crossing by Frank Waters
Three Cups of Tea by Greg Mortenson
West with the Night by Beryl Markham
Women Who Run with the Wolves by Clarissa Pinkola Estes
Your Truest Self: Embracing the Woman You Are Meant to Be by Janice Lynne Lundy

A Woman's Journey to God: Finding the Feminine Path by Joan Borysenko
Be Here Now by Ram Dass
Breathing Space: Mini-retreats For the Heart and Soul by Karen Ely
Crossing to Avalon: A Woman's Midlife Quest for the Sacred Feminine by Jean Shinoda Bolen
Dark Nights of the Soul by Thomas Moore
Don't Just Do Something, Sit There by Sylvia Boorstein
Enduring Lives: Portraits of Women and Faith in Action by Carol Lee Flinders
Everyday Zen by Charlotte Joko Beck
Expecting Adam: A True Story of Birth, Rebirth and Everyday Magic by Martha Beck
Faith: Trusting Your Own Deepest Experience by Sharon Salzberg
Goddesses in Everywoman by Jean Shinoda Bolen
Grace (Eventually): Thoughts on Faith by Anne Lamott
Growing Old Disgracefully by The Hen Co-op
Peace is Every Step by Thich Nhat Hanh
Reflections on the Art of Living: A Joseph Campbell Companion by Diane Osbon
Slow Love by Dominque Browning
The Buddhist Path to Simplicity by Christina Feldman
The Dance of the Dissident Daughter by Sue Monk Kidd
The Heroine's Journey by Maureen Murdock
The Invitation by Oriah Mountain Dreamer
The Seeker's Guide: Making Your Life a Spiritual Adventure by Elizabeth Lesser
The Seven Spiritual Laws of Success by Deepak Chopra
The Tao of Leadership: Lao Tsu's Tao Te Ching Adapted for a New Age by John Heider
The Tibetan Book of Living and Dying by Sogyal Rinpoche
The Way of Woman by Helen M. Luke & Marion Woodman
Traveling Mercies: Some Thoughts on Faith by Anne Lamott
Way of the Peaceful Warrior by Dan Millman
When Things Fall Apart: Heart Advice for Difficult Times by Pema Chodron
Wherever You Go There You Are by Jon Kabat-Zinn

Books to Take on a Women's Retreat to Awaken Creativity
A Room of One's Own by Virginia Woolf
Bird by Bird: Some Instructions on Writing and Life by Anne Lamott
For Writers Only by Sophy Burnham
Life's Companion: Journal Writing as a Spiritual Practice by Christina Baldwin
My Reading Life by Pat Conroy
One Continuous Mistake: Four Noble Truths for Writers by Gail Sher
The Right to Write by Julia Cameron
Three Dog Life by Abigail Thomas
Unreliable Truth: On Memoir and Memory by Maureen Murdock
Walking in this World by Julia Cameron
Wild Mind: Living the Writer's Life by Natalie Goldberg
Writing as a Way of Healing by Louse DeSalvo
Writing Down the Bones: Freeing the Writer Within by Natalie Goldberg

What should I bring on this retreat?

Food

We ask that all of our guests bring their own food, and enough personal supplies to be self sufficient. All participants in workshops are welcome to bring snacks and drinks along.

Shelter

Please bring a tent or shelter and comfortable bedding. Midian is a primitive campsite with a hot water shower house and running drinking water. Some campsites have access to electricity. These sites will be available on a first-come first-served basis. A suggested packing list for the retreat is available here .

Supplies

Bring along things that will help to nurture you during your retreat! Favorite foods, music, instruments, art supplies, and clothes that make you feel beautiful, comfortable, and special are encouraged. You may also choose to bring some items to contribute to our annual Goddess Shrine. All of your items donated to the shrine will be returned to you at the end of the retreat.

Vending

Vending is completely free with admission to the retreat. We encourage you to bring your wares to share for sell or barter. The retreat intends to support women's businesses and dreams. We can do this by sharing our gifts and prosperity with each other!

A Note to Breastfeeding Mothers

Our retreat welcomes you and your child with open arms. If you are not breast feeding we recommend that women leave their younger kids at home because sometimes we discuss mature topics, such as women's sexuality, childbirth, menopause, death and other subjects. If you are a new mother please let us know if you would like to participate in a special Mother's Blessing with your infant.

Pets

Midian isn't quite set up for pet camping yet, but it will be soon. If you need to bring a service animal with you, please know that you may do so. Otherwise, please leave your animals at home for now. They will be safer there.

Journals

We provide WGR journals to our participants. In the Spirit of conservation, we ask participants to bring their journals with them each year and fill the book before requesting a fresh one.

Amenities

Check out Midian's website for a full list of amenities.

Finally, please bring an open mind, a sisterly heart, and a playful spirit!

Notes

Notes

Culture and History of Our Retreat

First, Our Lexicon

I find it helpful in situations like ours to state what might seem obvious. That is, it might seem obvious to me, but it might not be obvious to you based on your experience, training, language use, etc. For that reason, I am going to explicitly define (within my limited and shifting ability to do so) some of the common terms that form the container for this retreat. Specifically, let's talk about the constituent parts of our event's name.

Woman - Any person who identifies in whole or in part as a woman and moves within their life in a way they find congruent with that aspect of their identity. We recognize that this single word is simultaneously simple, complicated, fluid, nuanced, and contested (especially here in the middle of the 2020's when gender-identity is wrapped up in political and culture wars). For us, though, the questions of "who is a woman" and by extension "who is this retreat for" are simple enough to address. Both cis-gender and trans-gender women are women. Period. And gender-non-conforming folks who want to sink deeply into women's space and women's experience for the weekend in order to connect with their feminine Selves and connect with a supportive community of women are women to us.

Goddess - We also use this term very inclusively, as we understand that not all cultures view their tutelary Spirits, genii locorum, cultural ancestors, and other BIG ENTITIES as Deities. Even more to the point, it is a very slippery slope to try to ascribe gender to these Spirits. The

19

"Goddesses" we call upon and learn about are typically perceived as female by the cultures where they are originally honored, but they may also have aspects, avatars, or stories that demonstrate gender-fluidity. (And by extension, we've called and honored Spirits who are typically perceived as male, but whose stories include transgender or gender-fluid themes and lessons.)

Retreat - An intentional act of taking time away from one's regular routine in order to renew, rejuvenate, replenish, and/or reconnect with oneself and/or one's community.

As I write this, I recognize that these are still very big concepts with a lot to unpack. That's actually built into our reasons for gathering. We spend time exploring together what it means to be a woman, how our experiences both reflect and define that womanhood, how Goddess stories teach and reveal the secrets (or Mysteries) of Divine Femininity, and what all of that means to us as individuals living this wild, magical, divine, and sometimes strange life.

This is a process of discovery. A process of inquiry. Answers aren't necessarily the goal for us, even though we ask LOTS of questions. Reflecting on our journeys and the wisdoms they hold for ourselves and each other is the "goal" — and also the process! And it is ever-evolving, ever-deepening, and ever-revealing.

Intention

We ask each woman who comes to the retreat to identify her own WHY. Why did you come? What are you hoping to get from this time away from your normal routines. We anticipate that we all came for one or both of the event's stated intentions — learning about ourselves, and/or learning about the Goddesses. But we recognize that our individual intentions can hold other goals and needs, as well.

Some women come to spend time with their sisters, mothers, daughters, and friends (like a reunion). Some come to find community and female friendships. Some women come to take a break from their typical obligations and duties so they can return to them renewed. Some women feel called to teach and lead ceremony or otherwise facilitate a healing and growth journey for the group. Some women come seeking validation and acceptance from their peers. Some women come to continue processing the trauma they have experienced as women among people who have a similar lived experience. Some women come to heal from bullying and isolation they've experienced at the hands of other women in other times and places. And sometimes, women come because they followed an intuitive call. They don't know what they need or want except to be in this space.

All of these (and more) are valid.

As facilitators of this event, we can't promise to deliver a specific experience. We can't guarantee the women who come to us will get exactly the thing they are looking for. But by giving them safe space and good tools, we can give them hope of finding it for themselves.

Presence and Participation

There have been a couple of years where women attended the retreat, but weren't actually "present." They set up camp with a friend or two, introduced themselves at one or two circle, and left (often while the retreat was still ongoing). For those women, I hope that their camping trip in safe space was the retreat they needed.

That is not typical of the Women's Goddess Retreat, though. And it isn't necessarily preferred by us for the overall experience of the retreat.

Stories are at the heart of our retreat process. Goddess stories. Your stories. My stories. Our shared stories. It is how we learn about the interior worlds of others, and it is a tool for making sense of our own inner worlds and outer experiences.

Nobody is compelled to share beyond their comfort level, but all are invited and encouraged to share because their stories and experiences and perceptions matter.

And all are encouraged and invited to participate in everything we do at the retreat. We want to actively include the women who haven't felt included among women in other times or other places in their lives.

There should never be exclusionary ceremonies or circles or gatherings within the parameters of this gathering.

All that being said, I hope it's obvious that I don't mean we have no private time or private thoughts. Nor that I'm implying that a small group of women applying self-care, soothing, or support to themselves or others can't self-define who is safe to bring into a very tight and intimate circle. Certainly, yes, those things happen and are needed.

We just want to avoid re-traumatizing each other by forming cliques and telling others "You can't sit with us."

Mostly Decentralized Leadership

The first year of this retreat was almost entirely the Natalie and Laurelei Show, in a manner of speaking. There were 13 Goddess Circles, with the two of us (alone or together as a couple) facilitating all but three or four of them. We proved the concept, pulled the community together, and created a working roadmap of what we wanted to experience. And we recognized before the first other women arrived that we never wanted to center ourselves — however much our theatre and public speaking backgrounds, our experiences as Priestesses within our spiritual community, or our roles as teachers and do-ers within that community might suggest otherwise.

Centering the leadership and facilitation of this retreat around any one or two women puts an incredible and unrealistic amount of pressure on those specific women, and it is disempowering for the rest who are relegated to the role of observer — and maybe as helper or assistant.

What a shame that would be, for all of us. What a missed opportunity for leaders and teachers and Priestesses to emerge or to arrive. What a recipe for disappointment. What a short lifespan this retreat would have had.

At the time of this writing, we are preparing for the 16th gathering of the Women's Goddess Retreat. Each Goddess Circle and Ceremony is facilitated by a different woman. Next year, the Opening and Closing Circles will be facilitated by different women, as well. We rotate and share these important roles, teaching each other how to hold space for the group, how to craft meaningful experiences, and how to handle the practical application of our spiritual principles.

I still handle most of the back-end — planning the schedule, processing registrations, managing the budget, coordinating communications. And this retreat is a legally or structurally considered a project of Asteria Books & Events, which is my company. But even these aspects of leadership have a plan for succession and delegation. And most decisions are discussed among an informal cadre of long-time participants and leaders.

No single one of us is the "sage on the stage." No single one of us is more expert than the others on what it means to be a woman in today's world. No single one of us has all the answers about how to facilitate community or ceremony or spiritual growth. We hold these things collectively, sharing the joys and the grief, the challenges and the growth.

Subrosa

Because we share our personal stories and experiences as part of our process, we are also sharing the thoughts and experiences that we hold closest to our hearts. Sometimes we hold them close and safe because their import is so personal and special and rare that it feels profane to speak them to anyone except the people who can relate to them based on their own experiences. Sometimes these thoughts and experiences carry grief, pain, or shame for us. Sometimes they reveal details about intimate partners, family members, or friends who are part of our stories.

In order to be vulnerable with each other, we have to know we are safe. We must know and trust that the private and possibly painful thing we shared won't be re-shared outside of the space. Outside the circle of our consent.

For that reason, we have adopted the term "Subrosa" and even hang a banner above our circle as a reminder that the personal experiences and thoughts shared by other women are sacred. The rose is the symbol of the sacred silence we offer each other. Our promise that their stories will not be used by us outside of the retreat.

Even with the best of intentions, we don't share another woman's story without her freely given consent to do so. And while it is understood that some women will have complicated social histories and possibly even strained connections to other women who are on the retreat, we expect the same level of consideration around privacy be afforded to everyone. Holding another women's experience as sacred, even when we don't personally "like" the other woman is part of how we heal the wounds of competition and conflict that are festering between women as a result of patriarchal stereotypes and agendas.

Let me give a couple of examples of inappropriate but well-intentioned sharing — and alternatives. (These names and stories are all fictionalized. Any resemblance of these to actual women who have attended the retreat is coincidental and unintentional.)

    * Sandra shared during a Persephone Circle that she was sexually assaulted by a man with whom she was in relationship. Callie knows the man and talked with a friend who wasn't at the retreat about Sandra's experience in an effort to reconcile the respectful and considerate image she has of the male partner with the story she heard from Sandra. Alternative: Callie could have initiated a general conversation with her other friend about the challenges of grappling with conflicting perceptions of a person in general terms, without mentioning or even obliquely referencing specific names, circumstances, locations, etc. Better Alternative: Callie could have journaled her thoughts during the retreat with a focus on understanding her own experience of perceiving these people, making decisions about who to trust and who to use caution around, or feeling conflicted about caring for a person who has perpetrated harm and trauma on another person. Even Better Alternative: Callie could have voiced during her own share-time that she believes and supports Sandra but is struggling to process this new information about a man she has viewed as a friend.

    * Janice is a Law Enforcement Officer. She went into law

enforcement to protect her community. She is a woman of color, and these two aspects of her identity are both among the reasons that she chose her career. Early in her career, she shot and killed a young man who drew a weapon on Janice's partner. The "weapon" turned out to be a very realistic-looking toy. She is still struggling with PTSD around this event, which she shared about during a Morrigan Circle. Yvette shared the story with her husband, who is a retired officer, hoping that her husband (who knows Janice socially) could be a support for Janice since he also took a life in the line of duty. Alternative: Yvette could have shared during her own share-time that she has some vicarious experience because of her husband's work and is open to helping Janice facilitate a supportive connection, if Janice wants that at this time.

Here's an example that is not so well-intentioned — along with an alternative.

    * Luna had a panic attack at the Lilith Circle in which the activity encouraged women to give voice to their rage. Many women chose to scream, which Luna wasn't prepared for. Her panic attack was witnessed by Iris, who doesn't particularly care for Luna (based on Luna's past relationship with one of Iris's close friends). At another community event, Iris tells that friend about Luna's panic attack. Alternative: Iris journals about her feelings toward Luna but simply says nothing to anyone about the panic episode. Even Better Alternative: Iris uses her journal or talks to a friend at the retreat who is already familiar with both situations to reflect on her own feelings, including exploring how she herself feels about Luna and working to separate those feelings from the ones she may have borrowed from her friend through their bonds of loyalty.

I'd love to say that this last sort of example would NEVER happen around our attendees, but the social training most of us come to the retreat with is a training that teaches us to tear each other down, rather than lifting each other up. This too is one of the foundational motivations for this retreat — that we actively work to undue to the programming that we've picked up from an over-culture that benefits from our conflict with each other.

We talk about these issues at length in our Opening Circle, and we hold every woman to the expectation that she will indeed honor the "Subrosa" nature of our work and play together. And in those rare cases where a woman violates that sacred confidentiality, we address it with her privately and decide together whether or not our retreat is a good fit for her. This is a compassionate response that gives her the respect and opportunity to change her behavior and examine the thoughts and patterns that created that behavior. These things haven't happened often, but in most cases, the "Iris" in this situation has sincerely apologized and made positive changes. In a few, though, the "Iris" hasn't returned to the retreat. And in a rare few, the "Luna" hasn't returned.

We don't want any woman to feel unwelcome, even when she has made an error in judgment. We are humans who are trying to be better, and it is impossible to grow if we are abandoned or discarded when we mess up. At the same time, we can't allow these behaviors to go unchecked because they are capable of eroding the safety of the space we strive to create and undoing the rest of the trust we are working to build with each other. If we allowed these sorts of betrayals to stand, we would eventually come to understand that the integrity of everything we have done is compromised.

As a person who is facilitating this retreat (or a retreat like this), it's also important to understand that you won't always know when these things are happening. Sometimes the woman whose trust was violated isn't aware. Sometimes when she is aware, she no longer trusts the retreat enough to come forward (and you might be the face of the retreat for her). That's a really hard reality of being in a community-based leadership role.

As a facilitator for this work, it's vital to stay open, communicative, and reflective. We have to process our own challenges and model how to do that for the women in our community. We have to learn how to care for ourselves and each other compassionately and ethically. It's a learning and growth process for us all, and we're always, always "doing the work."

Holding Space

One of the things that we do for each other at the retreat is "holding space" for ourselves and the women around us to engage in the deep work of the retreat. What does "holding space" even mean, though?

It means that we provide time, space, and some protocols for our attendees to safely explore things that may feel difficult, painful, vulnerable, private, etc.

Lots of factors go into our ability to hold space.

* The retreat has to establish the boundaries and expectations that women's stories are private, their feelings and experiences are valid and important, and that those of others are also meaningful and valid expressions of what it means to be a woman in the world today.

* Attendees need to understand that they themselves are part of the sacred container for the work we are doing and that their presence and attention matters. To that end, they are asked to stay present during the whole of share-time in each circle, that they only speak when they have the rattle/doll (our version of a talking stick), and that they not engage in side-talk when another woman is sharing.

* Sometimes a woman needs to continue processing her experience outside of the circle. This might be after the circle has ended, or it might be concurrent with the circle that is still ongoing. We encourage women to take the time they need, with the support they need. We only ask not to leave the main space in a disruptive way that deflects atten-

tion from the woman whose turn it is to speak.

Sacred Naps

We're tired. Women are exhausted. The statistics and stories around women's experience in the United States tell us that most of us work outside the home while still remaining the primary cook, caregiver, and housekeeper within the home. Most of us, then, have two full-time jobs. And that's not even considering the community involvements, kids' activities, and other hobbies and interests that we pursue for our own growth and fulfillment.

We are pooped.

Add to that the fact that we live in a culture that glorifies and praises exhaustion and vilifies rest, and it is no wonder that we are at a tipping point.

When Natalie and I read *Succulent Wild Woman* by SARK during the lead-up to the first Women's Goddess Retreat, we were both blown away by a little essay in that book titled "Waking Up (And then, taking a nap)." Here is what SARK taught us:

> None of us get enough naps. Naps are essential for mental health. Naps are productive — contrary to what we've been taught.
>
> Our culture promotes tension and crabbiness. Part of this is the severe lack of naps. Declare your home, or wherever you are, as a FREE NAP ZONE.
>
> I met a woman in her 70's who came up to me after a workshop

and said, "Thank you for giving me permission. My back is killing me. I'm going up to my hotel room and taking a nap! I have never done anything so self-indulgent. Isn't that sad?"

Plant and fly permission flags all over your life!

We have taken this idea one step further. We consider a woman's nap during this retreat to be a sacred act of self-care, and we not only encourage naps, but we applaud them.

Our presence in our Goddess and Ceremony circles is very important, but so is our personal self-care. So women are encouraged to really consider for themselves a single question at every opportunity for choice during the retreat:

"What would support my retreat intention?"

Sometimes that answer will be to engage in the activity with the group. And sometimes it will be to take time away from the group to honor yourself with Sacred Nap.

To be fair, we refer to ALL alone-time at the retreat as the Sacred Nap.

Journaling at your campsite? Sacred Nap!

Town run for chocolate? Sacred Nap!

Masturbating in your tent? Sacred! Nap!!!

As a Facilitator of this event, you are as entitled as anyone to your Sacred Naptime. As long as you are present at any Circle you have signed up to facilitate, you can absolutely duck out of group time or other circles to take your nap.

Courtesies and Considerations

We hold most of our circles and ceremonies in a space that is called the Main Pavilion. It is a covered shelter, not unlike the ones you see in state parks. Our chairs are assembled in one large, sometimes lopsided circle, and we spend the better part of 48 hours in this space together. Most of us eat our meals, drink our morning coffee, and chat until bed-time — all in this space.

There are a few courtesies and considerations that we offer each other to make this space as comfortable for everyone as possible:

* Smoking — There is no smoking in the main pavilion. Women who need to smoke are asked to step outside the space where they can still hear and participate the circles, handle their nicotine fix, and then come back to the circle. If multiple women choose to smoke at roughly the same time, they are reminded that we can still see and hear them, and are therefore asked to continue holding the space by refraining from chatter on the sidelines.

* Attention on the Speaker — If a circle or ceremony is being led, the Facilitator has the floor. Once "share-time" is initiated, the Facilitator will give the Goddess Doll (or rattle) to a woman, and the doll/rattle acts as a "talking stick." The woman with the rattle has the floor until she is ready to release the doll to her neighbor. We don't impose time limits on each other. We take the time we each need to speak, and we give each other the respect and courtesy of deeply listening to each other.

* "Twinkling" our Agreement — We seem to have adopted a gesture from somewhere that we call "twinkling." Instead of interrupt-

ing a woman who is speaking to say "Yeah, that happened to me, too" or "I agree" or "YES!", we hold our hands up (in front of us or above us), palms out, and just wiggle our fingers.

* Coolers and Picnic Baskets — We have not always had a caterer or food vendor to cook for us. One of the hacks we've developed is that a good number of us pack coolers and/or picnic baskets so we have easy-to-grab food and drinks right there in the main pavilion. I stash mine either in front of my chair or behind it.

DEI and Intersectionality at WGR

Diversity, equity, and inclusion are baked-into this retreat. We understand that we all have shared experiences as women, and that we have different experiences based on the facts of our lives and circumstances. We understand that we learn and grow together and that we all have valuable experience and insight to share with each other. And we also understand that women have identities beyond their woman-ness that impact their experience as women.

Race, cultural background, financial factors, mental health, mobility, sexual orientation — all of these impact us on deep, fundamental levels.

We want women to bring their whole selves to the retreat. That doesn't happen in a vacuum, though. We have to be intentional about embracing diversity, equity, and inclusion.

One of the measures we have recently taken to help with inclusion of women with disabilities is encouraging women to step up as "personal care assistants" to women with disabilities at the retreat. This can be a formal or informal arrangement. (Formally, the retreat is able to offer a discounted entry rate to a PCA who is attending with the main goal of helping an attendee with their self-care. Informally, it is as simple as being aware and on the lookout for a woman who needs help setting up camp, moving her gear, navigating the space, prepping her meals, or having something like a blood-sugar drop or panic attack — and then stepping up to help.

Financial Accessibility

It has been part of the ethos of this particular retreat to keep costs low in order for women with limited income the opportunity to participate. Most women's retreats are pricey — meaning that only women with substantial resources are able to attend.

Costs are rising, in general, and we understand that we will have rate adjustments over the years just to keep pace with the rising costs of venue rental, portable toilets, and supplies. However, it is important for us to find a balance so that our elders, sisters on a fixed income, and women who aren't necessarily being paid for their domestic labor can still come and get the retreat they need.

We offer discounted rates for our elders and our youth.

We have a few "work barter" opportunities.

And we can offer "scholarships" to women who reach out to us.

No woman is ever turned away due to lack of funds, and we have several long-time retreat attendees who pay for an extra ticket just to make those scholarships available.

If we round a corner one day and find that the retreat is no longer able to support itself, we will have to look at taking steps to shore up the financial deficit. That might mean raising rates. It might mean engaging in some fundraising. It might mean changing venues or looking for other ways to reduce costs.

What I hope it never means for this retreat is jacking up our prices to the point where our regular attendees can no longer afford to attend. It would be all too easy to look at other retreat models presented by online influencers and decide that $500 is a bargain compared to the $6,000 retreats that exist out there. (In 2024, the cost per adult entry to our retreat is $60 — a recent increase from the $50 that we began with in 2009. That fee includes the campsite, access to venue and amenities, and all of the content of the retreat from Friday through Sunday. It also includes an extra night of camping for women who want to arrive Thursday afternoon/evening.)

Trauma-Informed Space/Group

We've never been trained in trauma-informed care as a group. (Laurelei and some other Facilitators have been trained in this area as part of their professions, it is worth noting.) However, we've been holding the principles dear to our hearts since this retreat was born. Only recently have we had a name for this aspect of what we do.

Actually, Facilitators would be wise to explore some training in this area. Free options are available online, for those who are interested.

The basics, though, are pretty straightforward:

* a person can have trauma without a formal diagnosis

* a person can experience trauma as a result of an experience that may or may not be considered traumatic by another person also experiencing the same event

* no special degree or training is required to provide trauma-informed care

* growth and healing are possible after trauma

* the process of growth and healing can be non-linear

* we strive to provide safe space to process trauma without re-traumatizing the individual or the group

* healing of trauma happens on an individual level but often within a group environment

* no discussion or action is coerced or pressured

Some of our circles are light and joyful and celebratory. And some of them allow us the opportunity to explore and integrate the darkness and pain that we carry. Both are important. Both are needed.

We give our retreat attendees the opportunity to share those joys and those sorrows, but nobody is obliged to share beyond their comfort level. Indeed, nobody is obliged to share at all. The rattle/doll comes to each person who is present, but each woman decides for herself if and what she will share.

An important step in many women's healing journey is the simple discovery that they are not alone. We all deal with trauma on an individual level, but we are not nearly as isolated as that trauma tries to tell us we are. Just knowing that others have experienced something akin to our experience — and that they have survived, maybe even found a way to thrive — is empowering because it gives us hope.

Pandora, the first woman according to Greek mythology, is always with us. She'll help us unpack all of the woes and ills that we carry, but she also reminds us that HOPE is packed in, as well.

Food/Feast

Food has always been a rather tricky logistical aspect of our retreat.

We cap our registration at 35 total women in order to facilitate the flow of the content and give enough time to talk and process our experiences. But 35 customers isn't enough for most food vendors to justify the time and expense of setting up and prepping meals. For that reason, we've only had an on-site food vendor 6 of the 16 years of this retreat.

We may decide to add a catering option in the future, but that is a cost increase that most attendees don't favor at this time.

Our solutions, then, have been fairly organic, simple, and communal.

Most meals are handled in a "bring your own" capacity. We allow time for the group to break, go to town if needed, cook something at camp, or dig into one's cooler or picnic basket at the main pavilion.

There is a trend among many of us (started by me and Natalie in 2011 when I was faced with feeding myself, my then-11-year-old daughter who was attending for the first time, and Natalie —all while holding space and facilitating circles for the retreat as a whole). The trend is that we prep cold meals and room temperature snacks that we keep near us in the main space.

In the first couple of years, Natalie and I barely ate and we struggled to leave the main space because someone always seemed to need us — often in a priestess-capacity, but also sometimes just to handle purely logistical things. We learned a lot about caring for ourselves and each other, and the solution we came up with was what I call "cold camp cooking." In fact, it isn't cooking at all.

Many women have embraced this idea for themselves, as well. The retreat is a weekend away from their typical domestic responsibilities — not the least of which is the never-ending cycle of cooking and cleaning (which even in 2024 still falls to the women in the home).

The other food tradition that exists among us is a Friday evening communal meal. We all bring something to share with the group, and we eat together in the main pavilion space. We've got access to power, and the retreat gear includes 2-3 surge protector power strips so we can plug in the crock pots, roasting pans, hot plates, and percolators that give us access to hot food.

New in 2024, we have moved the retreat weekend away from the always-sweltering last weekend in August (before US Labor Day) to the highly-unpredictable climes of the first weekend October. Most of us felt that we could handle the chill better than the swamp. So also new in 2024 will be never-ending wassail, hot tea, and hot coffee, as well as Saturday chili and Sunday chicken & noodles. If it is well-received and not a huge hassle to prep and clean-up, we may make these hot offerings a staple of the retreat (or figure out a rotation of other warm comfort foods to further eliminate the burden of meal prep while keeping us all toasty and well-fed).

Safety

Our current venue, Midian Festivals and Events in southern Indiana, is a lovely space with a nice big parking lot outside of a heavy wooden double gate. For privacy and security, we keep the gate shut during the official hours of the retreat — Friday at noon to Sunday at 3pm.

Women are encouraged to park their cars somewhere inside the gated perimeter — usually close to their campsites. Some women who have mobility trouble also use their cars to transport them from camp to the main pavilion and back. And a few use their vehicles as camping spaces, as well.

Essentially, to the neighboring community, it looks like nobody's home while we're on the land. And that's great for us!

We have space within our budget for one (and not more than two) safety staff, but their role at this retreat is very different from working safety/security at festival-style camping events. Never once have our attendees gotten so drunk at our evening fires that they become belligerent and start conflicts with each other. Nobody has ever reported a sexual assault or bodily consent violation at our retreat.

The concerns we face are usually:

> * theft or damage to personal property. (One year, cars were tampered with in the parking lot. Another year, an attendee stole items from our unattended merch tables as we were packing out on Sunday. We moved the cars inside the gate, and the

light-fingered attendee was banned from returning.)

* accidents — like falls, fender-benders, etc.

Having one or two designated safety barters gives everyone a point of contact to help them trouble-shoot the problem before coming to the primary retreat Facilitator(s).

Typically, we ask our safety barters to take a walk through camping once or twice during the night to just make sure all is well. A stroll by the potties and showers is enough to let us know if someone has fallen or needs help.

Because we have an ethos around caring for each other as sisters, we tend to look out for one another. This means that safety personnel isn't truly needed at the retreat. (We like to keep the option open, though — and it gives us a reduced-cost option for a person on a tight budget who wants to help facilitate the retreat.)

If a situation arises that requires police, fire, or EMT intervention, call 911 and be prepared to meet the emergency responders at the front gate. (And see the First Aid section for more directions.)

First Aid

We keep a First Aid kit with us at the main pavilion at all times, and some of our Facilitators also keep one in their tent. We are only prepared to handle basic First Aid, and we keep a list of phone numbers and addresses for emergency services in the area, along with a printed set of driving directions.

At Midian, that looks like this:

911 — For all emergencies, but be very clear about our location, since it is unfamiliar to many in the area.

Location: 4093 Boone Hollow Rd near Springville.

Plus Code address: W85R+QG

Map coordinates: 38.909476, -86.658502

Directions from Springville:

Take IN-58 west out of Springville

Turn left to stay on 58-west

Drive past US Aggregates on the right

Turn left onto Armstrong Station Rd

Turn immediately right on Boone Hollow Rd

Midian is accessible from the first driveway on the right

If feasible, bring the individual(s) in need of emergency services to the front gate. This will limit the need of emergency personnel to navigate Midian's interior spaces, and it will be less traumatic and disruptive for the other attendees.

If that is not feasible, post someone to wait at the gate/road to escort the emergency responders to the location of the problem.

Be aware that if you call 911, ALL of the emergency services will show up — fire, police, and EMT.

It is vitally important that anyone working as a First Aid barter (and we typically only barter one person for this role) understands that if a situation can't be handled by our self-service First Aid kit, then that situation is beyond our capacity to handle. We can perform CPR and other stabilizing measures while waiting for help to arrive, but injuries and illnesses requiring treatment need to handled by medical professionals. There are both Urgent Care and Emergency Department facilities in Bedford, IN — about 10-15 minutes from our location.

Urgent Care — First Care Urgent Care — 2418 16th St, Bedford — 812-508-8683

Emergency Room — IU Health Bedford Hospital — 2900 16th St, Bedford — 812-275-1200

Notes

Notes

Structure of Our Retreat

There are basically three broad categories of content that are offered at the retreat:

>Opening and Closing Circles
>
>Goddess Circles
>
>Life Cycle Ceremonies

Opening and Closing Circles

These are the two circles that provide the framing for the retreat. The Opening Circle acts as an introduction, norm-setting, and ice-breaker, all of which help us transition into the retreat. And the Closing Circle gives us the opportunity to ground and center, gather feedback, and begin thinking about next year's retreat, all of which help us transition back to our daily lives and also provides continuity and connection from one retreat to the next.

It may be tempting as a Facilitator to give one or both of these "short shrift." Don't. They are both vitally important. In fact, attendees should be encouraged and reminded to plan their travel arrangements so they can be present for both of these. It is disruptive to both of these circles to have women driving their vehicles through the space, setting up/tearing down camp, etc while the group is engaging in the work. And it is much more difficult to create the emotional and psychological safety that is needed if there is a lot of movement and change happening among the participants.

These two circles do not involve calling on specific Goddesses, but they do both feature some aspects of ceremony.

In the past, these have been facilitated by a single Facilitator (most often Laurelei), but they could easily be co-Facilitated by multiple women (which is the direction we are moving, beginning in 2025).

Opening Circle Outline

Timing: Friday 12pm-2pm

Materials needed: Rattle/Doll, drum, journals, pens, check-in forms, QR codes for check-in and payment options, schedule copies

Procedure

    * Check-In — As women join the space, provide them with the QR code for online check-in and/or paper copies of the check-in form. Let them know that these need to be completed and turned in some time today (along with any registration fees they still owe). It is wise to have QR codes for any digital payments, as well.

    * Journals & Materials — Indicate where these are located. Remind women to use the same journal across multiple retreats, if possible. Provide a copy of the schedule for this year's retreat that they can either paste or copy into their journal. Indicate the location of pens, crayons, markers, etc. If there are coloring pages available this year, let them know these are available and can provide a "stim" or fidget for women who might benefit from something to do with their hands.

    * About Circles — Explain that we'll be working, playing, and meeting in circles throughout the retreat. Talk a little about the symbolism of circles with regards to equality, cycles, change, wholeness, and the Divine Feminine. Share that we believe that women's circles can change the world and discuss the "Millionth Circle" — the circle whose (metaphoric) formation tips the scales and shifts planetary consciousness. (This idea is explored in Jean Shinoda Bolen's book of the same name. This is a good one to have available in the Retreat Library.)

* Invoking the Circle — Perform a centering meditation. This can be any centering meditation that speaks to you this year. Following the meditation, invite everyone to join in chanting and drumming as a means of creating the sacred container for our work. Chants might include the following, but can also include improvisation and other known circle chants:

We are a Circle

Within a Circle

With no beginning

And never ending.

Spiraling into the center, the center of our beings

Spiraling into the center, the center of our beings

We are the weavers, we are the woven ones

We are the dreamers, we are the dream

We are the weavers, we are the woven ones

We are the dreamers, we are the dream

> Lady weave your circle bright
>
> Weave a web of dark and light
>
> Earth and Air and Fire and Water
>
> Bind us as One

We don't typically include Goddess chants here, but they are welcome, too, and might include:

We all come from the Goddess

And to her we shall return

Like a drop of rain

Flowing to the Ocean

Isis, Astarte, Diana, Hekate, Demeter, Kali, Inanna

* Welcome — After the group feels the circle is duly formed, offer a specific and intentional welcome. This could be as formal as a prayer or blessing, or as informal as saying "Welcome to the [2025] Women's Goddess Retreat." Also double check that everyone has a journal.

* About Retreats — Explain a little about the purpose of retreats in general, and about this retreat in particular. Talk about creating and maintaining the sacred container for the work. Share the group inten-

tions for this retreat and ask women to start thinking about their personal intentions.

* Structure of this Retreat — We will be exploring the stories and lessons of [x number] of Goddesses through storytelling, invocation, activities, reflection, and share-time. We will also be honoring women experiencing [x life transitions] as a way to celebrate the cycles of our lives. Anytime we finish a circle ahead of schedule, women are encouraged to sink into personal reflection and self-care.

* Norms, Culture, and Considerations — Explain the expectations our group has developed around:

- Presence and participation

- Subrosa

- Sovereignty, Self-Care, and Sacred Naps

- Smoking

* Retreat Library & Merch House — Explain that the "admin building" has been transformed for Friday and Saturday into a communal space for sharing of goods and books. One of the tables is marked as the Retreat Library. Books on that table are not for sale, but they are available to be loaned during the weekend. Women can contribute books by making sure their name is written in the front cover (and being sure to reclaim them on Sunday morning before the Great Goddess circle). And women can borrow books by signing them out (and returning them by Sunday morning — either to the table or their owner). Additionally, women who have brought goods to sell or trade can put their

items on a table along with a card or sign indicating payment info and options.

  * Wisdom Tent — Point out the Wisdom Tent and let women know that this is a quiet space for reflection, journaling, meditation, etc. It is a space to be "alone together" in quiet serenity. (The main pavilion, by contrast, is a noisier social space available to everyone between scheduled activities.)

  * Rattle/Doll & Share Time — Explain that everyone has an equal voice in the Circle. Emphasize the power of giving voice to your thoughts, feelings and experiences (both for yourself as a way to process, and also for others as a way to connect and make sense of things).Pass the doll/rattle for the first round of "Share Time" in which each attendee shares: their name and pronouns, a brief introduction, and their intentions for this retreat.

  * Wrap & Prep for first Goddess Circle — Thank everyone. Offer a blessing. Release to personal time until the next Circle begins.

Closing Circle Outline

Timing: Sunday 1pm-3pm

Materials needed: Rattle/Doll, drum, journals, pens,

Procedure

Seat women in a circle and thank them for coming.

Remind everyone to gather altar items, food, trash, and other gear from the shrine, main circle, and their camp.

Pass the rattle/doll for sharing time:

- Thoughts on the retreat
- Journal reading
- Free sharing

State how you hope that the Circle will be brought into the world by each woman.

Releasing the Circle:

- Centering meditation
- Chant with drum beat (invite improvisation)

    The Circle is open but unbroken

    The love of the Goddess is ever in our hearts

Merry Meet, and Merry Part

And Merry Meet again

Thank the women again.

Namaste mudra.

Release the Circle.

Goddess Circles

Most of the retreat revolves around our Goddess Circles. These always follow this Circle format:

* **Storytime** (with notes/facts/details) — Run time: between 5 and 30 minutes. This portion of the Circle should ALWAYS be directly related to lesson/theme. As a stylistic note, I would add that stories always seem to resonate more than a reading or recitation of facts about a Goddess. This is very much a "show, don't tell" scenario, if you're familiar with that reminder that is so often given to writers. Don't just tell us that a Goddess is associated with love, or competition, or motherhood. SHOW us how she loves by telling one of her love stories. Show us that she's a fierce competitor by relaying that famous foot-race she ran. Show us the lengths she went to in her nurturing of her children.

* **Invocation/Evocation/Prayer** — Run time: 1-5 minutes, typically. Women are encouraged to view and experience this "calling" of the Goddess in whatever way resonates with their spiritual practice. Call the Goddess to be present with us and help us to learn the lesson we see in her story.

* **Activity** — Run time: 10-30 minutes. Facilitators can get very creative with this portion of the Circle. The activity is intended as a way for us to experience some aspect of the lesson. You can get wildly creative here, but we ask that Facilitators not offer a guided meditation as the activity. We have a few reasons for this, but mainly, it's just too passive. It's also a little too easy to default to this passive activity, which can result in a very lopsided experience for attendees. In 2009, we had 13 Goddesses,

and something like 9 of the Circles featured a guided meditation. Facilitators should bring enough supplies for 35 women, if their activity calls for physical materials. (Also, if the Facilitator will need reimbursement for these supplies, the budget should be discussed ahead of time.)

* **Share Time** (pass the rattle, guiding prompt/question) — Run time: 60-90 minutes. The Facilitator will kick off Share Time with a guiding question of some kind. This can be as simple as "Tell us a little about what you experienced during this activity and how you feel that relates to this Circle's lesson." After posing the question, the Facilitator hands the doll/rattle to someone in the Circle and sits back down to participate in the sharing. Facilitators should allow at least 60 minutes for this — and more, if the lesson is heavy. Women are given space to talk as much or as little as they need without interruption. During this time, the Facilitator should feel free to process other women's shares exactly as she would if she had not been the one to facilitate the Circle. By that, I mean that she does not need (and indeed, should NOT) respond to each woman, control the flow of sharing, etc. The only thing she should be on the alert for is interruptions. (If an interruption happens, and the woman currently holding the doll/rattle seems unsure about reclaiming her time from the interrupter, then the Facilitator can intervene and redirect the focus on the woman who has the doll.) At the end of Share Time, the Facilitator reclaims the doll/rattle and brings a close to the Circle in whatever way makes sense to her. (Often, this conclusion takes the form of handing the rattle back to a designated retreat leader for housekeeping notes and reminders prior to a break for personal time.)

2009 Goddesses and Their Lessons

Shakti - Inner Awareness & Healing Ourselves

Diana - Owning Your Power & Finding Inner Strength

Hera - Dignity, Friendship, and Trust

Pele - Tending the Sacred Fire & Staying Centered

Gaia - Interconnectedness & Being Present

Aphrodite - True beauty & Self-Love

Babalon - Sexual Freedom & Bottomless Love

Hathor - Celebration & Sacred Movement

Triple Goddess - Women's Cycles & Change

Sophia - Inner Wisdom & Powers of the Sphinx

The Great Goddess - Charge of the Goddess & the Ultimate Boon

2010 Goddess and Their Lessons

Aphrodite - Pleasure & Joy

Athena - Peacemaking & deep Wisdom

Brigid - Mythic Resonance & Bardic Magic

Discordia - Celebration & Spontaneity

Hestia - Finding Sacred Space & Returning Home

Morrigan - Warrior Spirit & Healing from Trauma

Psyche - Heroine's Journey & Initiation

Sedna - Role-Shifting & Adaptation

The Great Goddess - Charge of the Goddess & the Ultimate Boon

2011 Goddesses and Their Lessons

Aphrodite - Pleasure & Joy

Brigid - Fire of the Forge & Creation

Cerridwen - Transformation & Sacred Cauldron

Grandmother Spider - Ancestors & Weaving Energy

Isis - Magic & Motherhood

Lilith - Empowerment & Selfhood

Santa Muerte - Death & Dissolution

Sekhmet - Ferocity & Temperance

The Great Goddess - Charge of the Goddess & the Ultimate Boon

2012 Goddesses and Their Lessons

Ariadne - Apotheosis through Ecstasy

Baba Yaga - Wisdom of the Elders & Strength of Self

Cybele - Diverse Sexuality & Acceptance

Inanna & Ereshkigal - The Heroine's Journey

Kali - Destruction & Creation

Pele - Tending the Sacred Fire

Shakti - Inner Awareness & Healing Ourselves

Shekinah - Our Divine Selves

The Great Goddess - Charge of the Goddess & the Ultimate Boon

2013 Goddesses and Their Lessons

Aphrodite - Priestesshood & Joy

Artemis - Wildness & Staying Young at Heart

Athena - Mentoring Widsom & Friendship

Demeter & Persephone - Mothers & Daughters

Hecate - Darkness & Mystery

Hestia - Kindling the Sacred Fire & Returning Home

The Great Goddess - Charge of the Goddess & the Ultimate Boon

2014 Goddesses and Their Lessons

Freya - Weaving Your Own Magic

Frigga - Compassion in Silence

Hella - Strength & Compassion

The Norns - Writing Your Own Destiny

Saga - Sharing Our Stories

Saadi - Knowing Yourself

The Valkyries - Courage

The Great Goddess - Charge of the Goddess & the Ultimate Boon

2015 Goddesses and Their Lessons

Eris - Self-Confidence & Chaotic Play

Grandmother Spider - Weaving Community

Hekate - Keys

Isis - Love & Loss

Labrys - Transformation

Lakshmi - Prosperity

Lilith - Freedom

The Great Goddess - Charge of the Goddess & the Ultimate Boon

2016 Goddesses and Their Lessons

Dionysus & Maenaeds - Gender Identity & Living Your Truth

Hera - Divine Drag

Kwan Yin - Compassion & Mercy

Macha - War & Knowing When to Fight

Psyche - Heroine's Journey

The Great Goddess - Charge of the Goddess & the Ultimate Boon

2017 Goddesses and Their Lessons

Athena - Deep Listening & Shared Wisdom

Kali - Personal Apocalypse

Nephthys - Closing Your Eyes & Trusting Your Inner Voice

Santa Muerte - Letting Go

Sekhmet & Hathor - Dance of Transformation

Queens of Heaven - Honey & Gold

The Great Goddess - Charge of the Goddess & the Ultimate Boon

2018 Goddesses and Their Lessons

Arianrhod - Bonds & Boundaries

Freya - When the Paint Falls Off

Grandmother Spider - Personal Fire & Weaving Connection

Pandora - Curiosity & Discovery

Rhiannon - Owning Your Magic

The Great Goddess - Charge of the Goddess & the Ultimate Boon

2019 Goddesses and Their Lessons

Aphrodite - True Beauty & Inner Light

Bast - Playfulness as Self-Care

Hera - Maintaining Self-Image through Crisis

Lilith - Letting Go

Oshun - Self-Love

Sacred Sisters - Flowing with the Work

The Great Goddess - Charge of the Goddess & the Ultimate Boon

2020 Goddesses and Their Lessons

Cerridwen - The Other Mother

The Fates - Spindle, Staff & Shears

Hel - Transformation & Aftermath

Ma'at - Personal Ethics & Boundaries

The Great Goddess - Charge of the Goddess & the Ultimate Boon

2021 Goddesses and Their Lessons

Mother Midian - Honoring Home

2022 Goddesses and Their Lessons

Brizo - Vision

The Erinyes - Righteous Rage

The Kharites - Creating Grace

Nott - Freedom

Selene - Darkness

Shakti - Shaping Spirit

The Great Goddess - Charge of the Goddess & the Ultimate Boon

2023 Goddesses and Their Lessons

Arachne - Weaving One's Own Tapestry

Brigid - Freeing Your Flame

Hekate - Self-Sabotage & Shadow Work

Loki - Identity

The Muses - Mystery & Memory

The Great Goddess - Charge of the Goddess & the Ultimate Boon

2024 Goddesses and Their Lessons

Athena - Standing in Your Power

Brigid - Creation & Creativity

Durga - Empowered by Our Ferocity

Echo - Confidence & Compliments

Nike - Just Do It

The Great Goddess - Charge of the Goddess & the Ultimate Boon

Examples in More Detail

2009 - Aphrodite - The Lessons of True Beauty & Self Love — Each woman was given a hand mirror and instructed to look at her face and find the beauty there. For those who struggled, they were given the option of listing a specific feature they could see as beautiful (like their eyes) or even a quality of a feature (like the golden flecks in their brown eyes).

2017 - Kali - The Lesson of Personal Apocalypse — Each woman was given a copy of a symbol called a Kali Yantra. They were instructed to color the symbol in any way they wanted. After they were finished they traded symbols with another woman. Everyone admired the handiwork of their partner for a minute or two, and then they were directed to destroy it.

2018 - Queens of Heaven - The Lessons of Honey & Gold — Each woman was given a bit of glittery gold sticker paper onto which she drew a sigil to represent herself (or some aspect of herself that she valued and admired).

Ceremonies

While rites of passage aren't celebrated every year, we do try to make time to honor the milestones that so often mark the various stages of a woman's life.

Here, you will find full scripts/outlines for each of the rituals we honor.

Shrine of the Great Goddess

I've come to think of this as the initiatory ritual of our Goddess community. It is essentially the same ceremony each year, but the results are different from year to year.

This ceremony, too, is a Goddess Circle.

The lesson is always the Charge of the Goddess & the Ultimate Boon.

I'm very torn about putting this ceremony/Circle in print, since (up to this point) we have always been very careful not to talk about it with women who haven't experienced it yet. We don't want to spoil the impact of that initiatory moment. If you are reading this handbook, though, you are probably a Facilitator already at this retreat, and have therefore experienced the Shrine of the Great Goddess — maybe multiple times. Or else you are looking to start your own retreat, and I would be doing you no favors by leaving out details.

So here is my compromise. I will give the details of how to perform the ceremony, but I will say nothing of what happens within the Shrine. (And that is perfect, too, since we don't give women instructions as they enter the Shrine. They are simply shown the way into the space. What they do while inside, and what they experience, is up to them — and the Great Goddess.)

Materials:

2-3 mirrors large enough to see one's face

2-3 tables

2-3 chairs

Items from the central altar

Water pitcher/bowl

Drums

Roles:

- Caller(s) — reads/recites the Charge of the Goddess by Doreen Valiente
- Water Priestess — lustrates each woman before they journey to the space
- Psychopomp — leads the women to the Shrine and back
- Guardian — stands guard outside the Shrine entry
- Music Leader — leads the chant and music in the main pavilion

Ritual Outline:

Women who have visited the Shrine at previous retreats are invited to help set-up the Shrine space and take ritual roles.

The Shrine is now established in the admin building that we have used as a library and merch room all weekend. Vending gear is removed from the tables, and 2-3 tables are arranged so that women arriving in pairs or triplets can each take a set in front of an altar space that features at least one central mirror and an arrangement of Goddess images and altar items.

The Caller explains that we will now be visiting the Shrine of the Great Goddess, where each woman will meet and have the opportunity to interact with Her. The Caller further explains that we will begin by invoking the Great Goddess, which will be followed by chanting and drumming. The chanting and drumming will continue throughout the entire Circle/ceremony, but women can rest their voices as needed, journal, etc. As women feel ready to approach the Shrine, they will queue in groups of either two or three (depending on how many altars are set-up) in front of the Water Priestess. The women are encouraged to ride-out the energy of the space and not dilute it for themselves or others by disengaging (talking, wandering off, etc.).

The Caller then reads the "Charge of the Goddess." In some years, we choose to have two Callers, with one reading the first half of the invocation, and the other reading the second half.

CHARGE OF THE GODDESS — by Doreen Valiente (as adapted by Starhawk)

Listen to the words of the Great Mother, Who of old was called Artemis, Astarte, Dione, Melusine, Aphrodite, Cerridwen, Diana, Arionrhod, Brigid, and by many other names:

Whenever you have need of anything, once a month, and better it be when the moon is full, you shall assemble in some secret place and adore the spirit of Me Who is Queen of all the Wise.

You shall be free from slavery, and as a sign that you be free you shall be naked in your rites.

Sing, feast, dance, make music and love, all in My Presence, for Mine is the ecstasy of the spirit and Mine also is joy on earth.

For My law is love is unto all beings. Mine is the secret that opens the door of youth, and Mine is the cup of wine of life that is the cauldron of Cerridwen, that is the holy grail of immortality.

I give the knowledge of the spirit eternal, and beyond death I give peace and freedom and reunion with those that have gone before.

Nor do I demand aught of sacrifice, for behold, I am the Mother of all things and My love is poured out upon the earth.

Hear the words of the Star Goddess, the dust of Whose feet are the hosts of Heaven, whose body encircles the universe:

I Who am the beauty of the green earth and the white moon among the stars and the mysteries of the waters,

I call upon your soul to arise and come unto me.

For I am the soul of nature that gives life to the universe.

From Me all things proceed and unto Me they must return.

Let My worship be in the heart that rejoices, for behold, all acts of love and pleasure are My rituals.

Let there be beauty and strength, power and compassion, honor and humility, mirth and reverence within you.

And you who seek to know Me, know that the seeking and yearning will avail you not, unless you know the Mystery: for if that which you seek, you find not within yourself, you will never find it without.

For behold, I have been with you from the beginning, and I am That which is attained at the end of desire

The Music Leader begins the drumming and chanting. There is only one chant for this Circle, which helps us achieve a very nice trance state.

> Ancient Mother, I hear you calling.
>
> Ancient Mother, I hear your song.
>
> Ancient Mother, I hear your laughter.
>
> Ancient Mother, I taste your tears.

The Water Priestess and the Psychopomp typically keep track of who has been into the Shrine and who is still waiting to go. Typically, the Water Priestess, Psychopomp, and Guardian are the last to enter the Shrine, during which time the Caller(s) and Music Leader might take up the roles of Water Priestess, Psychopomp, and Guardian for them.

When everyone has visited the Shrine, we stop chanting and the Caller passes the rattle/doll for Share Time. Women are encouraged to share:

- Thoughts on the Great Goddess
- Thoughts on their experience at the Shrine
- Musings on the Charge of the Goddess

After the last woman has shared, we take a quick potty break and reconvene with our lunches in tow for the Closing Circle.

Menarche Welcoming

Description:

Menarche marks a young adolescent girl's advancement into woman-hood. Menarche is a young woman's first menstrual period. Every woman has her own story of when and where this marker event occurred. In a healthy relationship, mothers and daughters both will anticipate a girl's menarche. It is generally the mother's role to prepare for her daughter's future menarche by educating her about her body.

Menarche is an important time in a young woman's life. Naturally the gathering for your daughter's rite of passage will be impromptu. Keep ready your list of nurturing women in your daughter's life to invite. Menarche is an excellent time for a girl to choose a Goddess as her first matron deity.

Menarche doesn't mean that womanhood has been achieved. It is simply the next step from girlhood into womanhood. Womaning rituals can be held for young women who have reached that precarious time when they begin to leave the nest.

How might it have been different for you,

if, on your first menstrual day your mother had given you

a bouquet of flowers and taken you to lunch

and then the two of you had gone

to meet your father at the jeweller,

where your ears were pierced,

and your father bought you your first pair of earings,

and then you went with a few of your friends

and your mother's friends

to get your first lip coloring;

and then you went,

for the very first time,

to the Women's Lodge,

to learn

the Wisdom of the Women?

How might your life be different?

-- Judith Duerk, Circle of Stones

This ritual was originally developed by Natalie Long, co-founder of the Women's Goddess Retreat. It was first performed in 2011.

Materials:

Journal prompt for the girls:

> What are your thoughts and feelings about joining the circle of women? About getting your period? About growing up?
>
> What do you hope the future will bring you?
>
> What name would you like to be known by while in the women's circles of this community?

Rattle/Doll

Journal and pens

Procedure:

The girls are separated from the main circle. They are seated in the woods alone and asked to reflect on the questions above and to meditate.

The Circle is cast.

The Goddesses are called. The women present are invited to call upon those Goddesses whom they would like present for the rite, as are the Goddesses most dear to the girls undergoing the rite.

The women present share stories about growing up, experiencing menarche, their hopes for themselves at that time in their lives.

The mothers of the girls join their daughters in the woods. Each mother ties a red ribbon to her daughter's wrist and connects it to her own. They share private advice and wisdom before leaving this separate place.

Mothers and daughters approach the Circle.

Guardian asks the girls their names. The girls each respond, "I am _____, daughter of _____, and my name among this community of women is _____."

Guardian challenges each girl in turn before allowing admission to the Red Tent and the Circle of women.

Guardian says "The Red Thread, of which you now bear a token, is a symbol with may layers of meaning. One of those layers has to do with ancestral lines, like the mitochondrial DNA that links us back to our mother's mothers to the very dawn of our species. The lines of our heritage are carried in our blood, and the moon blood that has manifested within you in another red thread that connects you to the cycle of birth and life. Mothers, are you prepared to allow your child to grow into a young woman? (Allow a moment for their response.) Daughters, will you retain the link to your mother even though the bonds of childhood are forever changed? (Allow time for their response.) "

Guardian cuts the red ribbons. "Under the protection of the Goddess, welcome to the Circle of women. Take your place among us."

Everyone cheers!!!

Girls draw a Goddess card and are asked to speak about their time in the woods.

Gathered women offer advice, stories, and gifts.

Cake is shared. (Red velvet is a favorite for this!)

Circle is dissolved.

Womaning (Coming of Age)

Description:

"You are growing up so fast!" say all of your mother's friends, but to you it feels like the transition into womanhood has taken a lifetime. It has. Now you stand on the edge of the circle of women, ready to be admitted as an equal into their community of sisterhood. These women gaze at you with mist in their eyes. They can still see the little girl who picked flowers for them and danced in the rain. They can also see the radiant beauty that you have become as a young woman. They know that the journey is hard. There will be tears. There will be pain. There will be loss. Such is the way of all women. But you must come into their circle, for there will also be joy, and new life, and growth beyond reckoning.

You are the Maiden at her peak, full of juicy lust for life, pure potential. Come now, and enter the circle of women. Take your place by your mothers, sisters, and grandmothers. Hear the wisdom that they have to share with you. Feel the love that they pour out for you. Take your place in the eternal circle.

This ritual was originally developed by Becca Davis, one of the inaugural members of the Women's Goddess Retreat. It was first performed in 2010. (This ritual is reconstructed based on the format Becca used. No copy of Becca's original ritual exists.)

Materials:

Water bowl

Anointing Oil

Red wine, pomegranate juice, and cups

Gifts

Cake/treats

Roles:

Mothers (Can be adoptive or spiritual mothers.)

Mentors

Psychopmp

Guardian

Water Priestess

Procedure:

The young women are segregated with their mothers while the Circle is prepared. The mothers and daughters use the time to talk about some of the early adult experiences the younger woman has already experienced, her goals and hopes for her adult life, and her questions and worries as well.

While this reflection is happening, a space is prepared for the ordeal. This ceremony can happen in the main Circle space, if chairs and other objects are moved and blankets are placed in the "birthing" area. Alternately, it can happen in a grassy or sandy area. The women of the circle move into position, forming two lines that face each other. Women can stand, kneel, or sit in a chair to participate. They will form a tunnel that gently but firmly squeezes and pushes on the sides and backs of the young women as they crawl from one end to the other.

When the Circle is prepared, a Psychopomp is sent to bring the first mother and daughter back to the space. The young woman is blindfolded before they make the journey and must trust her mother to guide her back to the ritual space.

As they reach the Circle, the young woman is challenged by a Guardian. "The passage into this next phase of your life is long, winding, and filled with challenges. It is a birthing of yourself to yourself. Like a baby in the womb, the time has come for you to make your way into a new freedom and a new experience. Are you prepared to trust the mother who has brought you this far, your chosen mentor, and this Circle of women as you make this transition?" (Wait for their answers.) "Then it is time to begin."

The Water Priestess pours some water from her bowl over the young woman's head. "In the waters of birth are you baptized."

Mother helps her daughter to her knees and guides her to the opening for the tunnel. She says, "Make your way through as best you can."

The women of the Circle gently but firmly push and squeeze the young woman as she crawls through the tunnel. It is okay to make the passage difficult, forcing the young woman to work and struggle, as long as care is taken not to hurt her in the process.

While this is happening, the girl's mentor is stationed at the tunnel's exit. The mentor says words of encouragement and direction to help the young woman navigate her ordeal.

When the young woman reaches the end and is out of the tunnel, her mentor helps her to her feet, removes the blindfold, and hugs her mentee.

Guardian says, "Welcome, Sister!"

The Water Priestess anoints the young woman with oil.

The young woman and her mentor take their place with the group.

If there are multiple young women undergoing the ceremony, the process is repeated. Once everyone has been "born," all women move back to their place in the Circle.

Young women draw a Goddess card and are asked to speak about their time in the woods.

Stories and advice are shared. Gifts are given. Red wine and/or pomegranate juice is shared. Cake or other treats are shared.

Circle is dissolved.

Blessingway (aka, Pregnancy Blessing)

Description:

Life grows within you, woman. Your stomach swells with potential, with abundance. You are ripe, you are a Goddess. You can sense the deep link within you to eternity. You can sense your umbilical cord stretching back, far past your grandmother, into pre-history and forward forever and forever into future generations.

It is right and good to celebrate this time. You may have baby showers, yes. You may hear birth stories from older mothers, women who have bravely been to the birthing bed before you. Perhaps you have been there before as well.

Wouldn't you love to honor the spiritual component of this special time? Do you long to hear your sisters sing to you and your growing child, to bless your womb with life, light, and love, to honor the transition you are making into motherhood? Come into the circle, woman, and listen to the song we have to sing for you and your child.

Woman
You are the Earth Mother
your thighs are meaty

and can hold you proud

Woman
you are the Earth Mother
Giver of life
Bringing forth miracles from thy womb

Woman
you are the Earth Mother
Look into the mirror
and see why the children adore you

Woman
You are the Earth Mother
You are She
and I am Me

Bare thy breasts proudly
to the moon
Oh wonderful woman!

by: Mandie (as posted at http://www.yoni.com/motherf/
barebreasts.shtml)

This ritual was originally developed by Laurelei Black, co-founder of the Women's Goddess Retreat. It was first performed in 2015.

Materials:

Cloth pouch to hold talismans

Talismans and amulets of protection, health, and blessing (brought by women present — or items for crafting a talisman)

Water

Honey

Milk

3 colors of Perle cotton thread or natural fiber yarn (in shades of blue)

Roles:

Facilitator

Caller

Music Leader

Weaver

Water Priestess

Procedure:

The expectant mother (or group of mothers) is brought into the middle of the Circle and given a comfortable place to sit.

Facilitator talks a little about the joys and worries of pregnancy. Explains that we are going to focus our energy on blessing and protecting the Mama and Baby in our midst.

A Caller invokes Goddesses of pregnancy and childbirth — such as Brighid, Demeter, Artemis, Frigga, etc. Special care should be given to calling the Mama's primary Goddess, if she has one. Other women in the Circle might add the Goddesses they associate with pregnancy and childbirth, as well.

Facilitator explains that we'll be braiding a pregnancy protection cord for Mama to wear throughout the pregnancy, as well as building a charm bag for her to carry or keep on her altar at home. We will do all of this while singing to Mama and Baby, offering our own personal words of blessing, and anointing her with milk, water, and honey — for nurturing, easy birth, and sweetness along every step of the journey. Talisman materials should be available for women who are not braiding to fashion and empower a charm as we continue the Blessingway.

The Weaver passes the threads/yarns around the Circle so that everyone has a chance to braid at least a little of the braid. This works best when a bobbin system is used to bundle the long threads to help prevent tangling. It is also beneficial to have one woman hold the head of the braid while another woman is braiding her particular section. The Weaver can be the one holding the head — or she may just stay near the cords as they are plaited to help untangle knots and focus the collective energy into them.

While the braiding is happening, the Circle moves fluidly and organically between singing, chanting, and storytelling. Women are encouraged to share stories of the joys, hopes, uplifting surprises, and helpful advice they experienced in their own pregnancy and birthing experiences. When stories fall silent, the Music Leader can lead another round of chants or start singing a song about pregnancy, birth, or infants. (Note: These songs can be pulled from any musical tradition, not just "Pagan songs/chants."

Sometimes more difficult or challenging stories bubble up to the surface, as well. No woman should be shut down or silenced, but the Facilitator or Ritual Team should gently transition the story to the reminder that

THIS is why we seek protection for both mother and child. THIS is why we want to wrap them in blessings. Mama and Baby both have hard work ahead of them that isn't without its dangers. But we are actively working to encircle them both in our love, protection, and blessings.

While the braiding, singing, and storytelling are happening, women will approach the Mama and offer her words of blessing and a talisman or amulet to bless the child. (The talisman goes into the bag, which Mama will place on her altar at home.) They will finalize the blessing by pouring a small amount of milk, water, or honey into a bowl.

When the cords are ready, and the charm bag is full, the Water Priestess will dip her finger into the sacred bowl and use the fluid to anoint and seal the cords, charm bag, and body of the Mother. Any remaining fluid is given as an offering by the Mother to the Goddesses who have taken part in the Blessingway.

The cords are tied around Mama's belly and she is told to wear them under her clothes as often as she can until it is time to deliver. When her midwife or doctor indicates the time has come to push, her partner can cut the protection cord.

After the delivery, the cut protection cord can be added to the charm bag and kept on the Baby's altar.

Birth Blessing

Description:

From your womb has come a new life. From your breasts flow rich milk to nourish that life. From your hands pulse gentle energy ready to caress and defend your child. From your mouth flow songs to comfort and words to teach. Now you are a mother. No longer is your heart completely your own, for now it lives and beats outside of your body.

Maybe you are a first-time mother. Maybe you have given birth before, but seek affirmation for yourself within the circle of women and blessings for your newest family member.

Let our community welcome your child by the name you have gifted it with. Let us shower them with gifts of blessing and protection, like fairy godmothers. Let us hold you close and rejoice that you have bravely undergone the awesome initiation of giving birth! Join with the other mothers of the Circle and receive their blessings. Share your story of pain and triumph. Feast joyfully knowing that you will magically transform that food into milk for your child.

Celebrate life! Celebrate motherhood!

Ancient Mother

Ancient Mother, I hear you calling

Ancient Mother, I hear your song

Ancient Mother, I share your laughter

Ancient Mother, I taste your tears

O la mama, wa ha su kola

O la mama, wa ha su wham

O la mama, kow wei ha ha ha ha

O la mama, ta tay kaiee

Ancient Mother, I hear you calling

Ancient Mother, I hear your song

Ancient Mother, I share your laughter

Ancient Mother, I taste your tears

This ritual was originally developed by Laurelei Black, co-founder of the Women's Goddess Retreat. It was first performed in 2015.

Materials:

Cloth pouch to hold talismans

Talismans and amulets of protection, health, and blessing (brought by women present — or items for crafting a talisman)

Treats (cupcakes, fruit, etc)

Roles:

Facilitator

Mama

Baby

Caller

Procedure:

Mother and Baby are given a seat of honor within the Circle.

Facilitator says: "Sisters, one of our own has done a thing both miraculous and mundane. She has brought forth a new life, a new member of our community!" (Everyone cheers!) "We are gathered here to welcome this child, praise this mother, and celebrate the continuity of the circle of life."

Caller invokes Goddesses of motherhood, paying particular attention to the primary Goddess of the Mama. Others in the Circle are invited to speak the names of Mother Goddesses they revere.

Facilitator asks Mama to introduce her baby to the group, using the name she has chosen for the child. Facilitator says to the child: "Welcome, little _____, to the world and to this community of women."

Circle of women shares stories, advice, and words of blessing. Cake or other treats are shared.

Talismans are made and empowered and placed in the charm bag for Baby. Like fairy godmothers, women can speak aloud the blessings they are attaching to their charms.

If anyone brought gifts for Mama or Baby, they can be given now.

Circle is dissolved after gifts and blessings are bestowed.

Queening Rite

Description:

You are suddenly have hot flashes. The kids have left home (or maybe they've just returned!). You're re-evaluating your whole life... and you are absolutely certain that you are not ready to be a crone. Congratulations! You've just become a Queen!

As women are living longer a new face of the "Triple" Goddess has emerged. The average woman's lifespan is now 80.8 years in the United States. That means that even if 20 years time is devoted to each phase of a woman's Maiden-Mother-Crone cycle, there is still an extra 20 years after the motherhood cycle is "over" before cronehood begins. These are the Queen years, the time when a woman comes into her own power and is in control of her own life.

Think about it. You are not responsible for your children anymore. You are not responsible for anyone but yourself. You are the Queen of your own life, and, honey, you deserve a crown!

In our opinion you are now in transition between the phase of the Mother and that of the Wise Woman. Maybe you haven't stopped bleeding, but your body has begun to make the shift that way. Prehaps you are also feeling a transition in your life emotionally or intellectually or spiritually, too—not just physically. You may be pausing, looking back on your life, reevaluating what you want out of your life and making plans for your future. But transition times can be confusing, chaotic and scary.

Our culture's view of menopause is pretty negative, but in ancient, female-honoring cultures, menopause was considered sacred, along with the other blood mysteries of women—childbirth and menstruation. In fact, the word "blessing" comes from an old English word meaning "bleeding." Since women could miraculously bleed and not die, menstrual blood was connected with longevity and immortality, healing, and fertility.

So, let's have a ritual to help initiate you into this new phase of being. Become the mistress of the hive, taste the honey-sweetness of sovereignty. Let us crown you as the Queen you are.

This ritual was originally developed by Natalie Long, co-founder of the Women's Goddess Retreat. It was first performed in 2017.

Materials:

Crimson Robe

Throne

Gold (or Star-Strewn) Canopy with four poles

Anointing Oil

Orb

Scepter

For each Queen: Crown, Ring, Stole

Roles:

Guardian

Hierophant

Herald

Water Priestess

Psychopomp

Procedure:

The new Queens are asked to relax and talk amongst themselves. While those who are already Queens in our Circle prepare the space. They are also asked to determine an order amongst themselves. (They can use any criteria that seems fitting to them: age, birth-month, height, recency of menses, years of retreat participation, etc)

The psychopomp brings the first Queen to stand before the throne, where she faces the Hierophant.

Oath

Hierophant: Will you, _____, solemnly promise and swear to be true to yourself and the work that you were created to do above all other things, and to rule yourself with a heart full of Love?

Queen: I swear.

Anointing Hands, Head, and Heart

Water Priestess: May these hands work only for the Highest Good.

May this mind be filled with Wisdom and Understanding.

May this heart be blessed with Love and Laughter.

Presentation of the Stole and Crimson Robe

Hierophant: Gird yourself always as a Warrior, a Priestess, and a Servant to nothing but Love.

You are wrapped in the protection of the Goddess, and she will guard you in your ways.

Psychopomp seats Queen at Throne under a Golden (or Starry) Canopy.

Presentation of Crown Jewels (Orb, Ring, and Scepter)

Hierophant: This golden orb is a symbol of your dominion over your world, and the triumphing of your goals. Upturned, it is the symbol of womanhood. It symbolizes that only you can create the world that you envision.

Hierophant: This ring is a symbol of love and fidelity to yourself. Let no one break the magic circle of its promise.

Hierophant: This scepter is the rod of Justice and Mercy. Anciently, it was used as a measuring tools and a keeper of time for female cycles. May discernment guide you towards Wisdom that you may find a measure of balance in all that you do.

Crowning with Declaration

Hierophant: This crown, which you have chosen to symbolize your ascension from the sacrificial era of Motherhood into the radiance of Queenship, must always be born with regal gait, lest it fall from its perch.

Hierophant: Therefore, let there be beauty and strength, power and compassion, honor and humility, mirth and reverence within you always.

Herald: Ladies, it is my honor to present to you Queen _____ of House _____, the first of her name!

All: "Hail Queen _____! Goddess save the Queen!" X 3

Those who wish to swear fealty may do so now.

The Queen takes her place among the Circle as each successive Queen is crowned.

Circle is dissolved.

Wise Woman Rite (Croning)

Description:

The Crone's title was related to the word crown and she represented the power of the ancient tribal matriarch who made the moral and legal decisions for her subjects and descendants. It was the medieval meta-morphosis of the wise woman into the witch that changed the word Crone from a compliment to an insult and established the stereotype of malevolent old womanhood that continues to haunt elder women to-day. ~ Barbara Walker, The Crone

Patti Wigington says:

In early cultures, the female elder was considered a wise wom-an. She was the healer, the teacher, the imparter of knowledge. She mediated disputes, she had influence over tribal leaders, and she cared for the dying as they took their final breaths. For many women in Pagan and Goddess-centric belief systems, reaching the status of Crone is a major milestone. These women are reclaiming the name of Crone in a positive way, and see it as a time to joyfully welcome one's position as an elder within the community.

Rachel Patterson writes:

The word crone is derived from the word cronus (time) and it means the wisdom gained through life long experiences. Krone also means crown. To become crowned crone then, acknowledges that you are a wise woman who has gathered up the fruits of her experience into profound and sovereign understanding. The wise crone becomes the resource of wisdom for her community and a source of inspiration for her circle of cronies.

Patti Wigington adds:

For a long time, to be called a crone was an insult. The very word implied a wrinkled, hunchbacked old woman, unwanted and unloved. Women who had reached an advanced age were dismissed as useless hags, and there was nothing to celebrate about it at all. Fortunately, times are changing, and more and more women are welcoming this aspect of their life. We spend many years in the guise of the Maiden followed by a couple of decades as Mother for many of us. Why not celebrate this next phase of life?

(The source/author for this next passage is unclear. We didn't write it – as you can guess by the British English spelling conventions, but it was on our original website for years.)

Whether you embraced the Crone stage from the moment you had your first hot flush (aka hot flash or power surge) or whether you reluctantly dragged your feet into Cronedom, there is often a feeling of regret that there was never any definite moment when you could mark the occasion. Many women feel that they have somehow been cheated out of the acknowledgement that they have moved forward and now have new status. In the past - and indeed in some cultures still today – the onset of menstruation is recognised by a special ceremony for the young girl in which she is admitted to the circle of women. At the other end of the spectrum, it was believed that when a woman stopped menstruating, she kept her wise blood inside her and increased her wisdom. Elderwomen were, therefore, revered and honoured. The Croning Ceremony aims to provide a ritualised acknowledgement and celebration of a woman's move forward into her Cronehood and wisdom. It doesn't matter whether you have only just started the menopause or whether it happened several years ago: what matters is that you want to mark this rite of passage.

You've probably heard the cliche, "Life isn't about the destination but about the journey." These words take on a more profound meaning in the crone years. Life is more about a continuous journey of experiences, lifelong learning and growth, both spiritual and human. The crone is a woman that is gracefully adapting to the process of aging. She quietly inspires others. She is comfortable in her own skin and with her spirituality. Her intuitive and creative powers are pronounced. But what really sets the crone apart is that she embodies a passion to explore meaning in her life; and she exemplifies an unselfish willingness to share her honesty, knowledge, wisdom, love, and compassion.

Crossing the threshold into Cronehood can be a major event in a woman's life. It's a celebration of all that you've learned, and all that you will come to know in the future. For many women, it's a time to make new commitments and vows. If you've ever had an interest in taking a leadership position in some aspect of your life, now is a great time to do so. This third cycle of your life is the one in which you become an Elder, and you've joined a special group. You have a lifetime of achievements behind you, and decades more to look forward to. The word Crone should now be a word of power for you, so celebrate it. You've earned it.

The Charge of the Crone

I am the Queen of Magick and the dark of the Moon, hidden in the deepest night. I am the mystery of the Otherworlds and the fear that coils about your heart in the times of your trials. I am the soul of nature that gives form to the universe; it is I who awaits you at the end of the spiral dance. Most ancient among gods and mortals, let my worship be within the heart that has truly tasted life, for behold all acts of magick and art are my pleasure and my greatest ritual is love itself. Therefore let there be beauty in your strength, compassion in your wrath, power in your humility, and discipline balanced through mirth and reverence.

You who seek to remove my veil and behold my true face, know that all your questing and efforts are for nothing, and all your lust and desires shall avail you not at all. For unless you know my mystery, look wherever you will, it will elude you, For behold, I have ever been with you, from the very beginning, the comforting hand that nurtured you in the dawn of life, and the loving embrace that awaits you at the end of each life, for I am that which is attained at the end of the dance, and I am the womb of new beginnings, as yet unimagined and unknown.

This ritual was originally developed by Laurelei Black, co-founder of the Women's Goddess Retreat. It was first performed in 2023. (It is worth noting that Hetty led the first Croning Rite to happen at WGR in 2010. However, no copy of that original ritual exists.)

Materials:

Cauldron

Cloak

Staff

Cauldron

High Seat (throne, chair, place of honor)

Roles:

Herald

Hierophant

Guardian

Water Priestess

Psychopomp

Procedure:

Presenting the Wise One ~ The Wise One stands as the Herald announces: "Today, we celebrate and honor [Name], whose wisdom and experience have marked them as an Elder among us!" (Everyone cheers.)

Cloak ~ The Hierophant drapes the Cloak over the shoulders of the Wise One. "Wisdom is often veiled. Wisdom is a shield and a comfort. Wisdom is a mantle of responsibility and honor."

Staff ~ The Guardian hands the Staff to the Wise One, who holds it in their right. "Wisdom is a support. Wisdom is a tool. Wisdom is a weapon."

Cauldron ~ The Water Priestess places the Cauldron into the left hand of the Wise One. "Wisdom is a sustenance. Wisdom is a medicine. Wisdom is a mystery."

High Seat ~ The Psychopomp leads the Elder to the High Seat. Before the Elder sits, the Hierophant says, "By this robe, this scepter, and this cauldron, we recognize and honor you as a Wise One among us — one who has learned many hard truths and tasted many joys and many tears. We honor you as an Elder of our Sisterhood — a counselor and friend. Take, now, this place of pride and receive our thanks." The Wise One sits in the throne/chair.

Presentation of Gifts and Advice ~ The Hierophant invites the assembled community to offer their gifts (which includes their service, blessings, and thanks — only other Wise Ones should offer wisdom about this stage of life) to the Wise One. Everyone is given the opportunity to speak, if they choose.

Red Rose ~ The Hierophant presents the Wise One with the red rose (which can be fashioned as a talisman to be worn or carried, or as a talisman to reside on the Elder's altar). "Red Roses have many meanings among the Wise. One of those Mysteries is explored each year at this retreat -- Subrosa. I give you this emblem, which is blazoned on our banner, to contemplate as you continue on your journey, along with my blessings and the blessings of our Goddesses."

Crossing Rite (Funeral/Memorial)

Description:

When a member of our community passes into Spirit, our Circle comes together to mourn our loss and honor their life. These are hard but vital moments for us as a community. By honoring even this most challenging station in the cycle of Life, we are able to hold close those who have continued on their journey, and we are able to make space in our Spirits for the transition we know eventually embraces us all.

This ritual should be held on Saturday evening at the main bonfire field as the last Circle of the day.

This ritual was originally developed by Laurelei Black, co-founder of the Women's Goddess Retreat. It was first performed in 2024 in memory of Becca (Firehorse) and Bonnie, who were also honored together at our first Wise Woman Rite.

Materials:

Small wooden box with latch

Coins

Cauldron

Tealights, light

Fire, firepit

Libations, cups

Altar table

Photos and mementos of the Beloved Dead

Note cards for messages

Roles:

Facilitator

Fire Keeper(s)

Cup Bearer

Purse Warden

Procedure:

Gather the women in a Circle around the firepit, where a fire is laid and is already burning.

An altar for the Beloved Dead is constructed somewhere between the fire and the Circle. Upon it are placed all of the ceremonial items, including the photos and mementos of the Beloved Dead.

Farewell (Facilitator): "Beloved Sisters, we have come together today to join in both mourning and celebrating. We mourn our loss of [Decedent] while celebrating the life she lived among us. I invite any who are moved to speak their farewells aloud and give voice to their grief." All who wish to speak are given leave to do so.

Burning of Messages (Fire Keeper): "Some things we might want to say are just between us and the Sister who is now in Spirit. If you feel so moved, write your message on a card, bless it, and burn it in either the cauldron fire or the bonfire." Fire Keeper assists, as needed, for safety.

Coins for the Crossing (Purse Warden): "Souls sometimes linger during this time of transition, and so it is an ancient custom across many cultures to provision the Beloved Dead for their journey. Bless your coin with your hopes for our Sister's journey with the stars. I will bear this casket around our Circle as you pay your respects. After our ceremony ends, this cask will be housed at Ancestor Shrine, where its contents will aid our friend on her journey." Coins can be provided to anyone who doesn't have one of their own.

Toasts to Life and Death (Cup Bearer); "Mourning and grief are a natural part of Death, but we have also come to celebrate the Life of our friend and Sister. We choose to remember the joys, the love, and the vitality she imparted during her time among us. Let us raise a cup and share our stories as a testament to a life well and fully lived."

Stories are shared freely. When they come to a natural stopping point, the Facilitator should invite the women to share food, more drinks, and dancing around the fire. More stories will naturally comes, as will both tears and laughter. The ritual team should be prepared to hold space for each other and all the women assembled.

Before retiring to bed, the ritual team should carry the box of coins along with any other offerings that were left to Ancestor Shrine, with due reverence and mirth.

Notes

Administrative Bits

This retreat requires very little in terms of administrative fussery — all things considered. (Compare what is listed here to the Asteria Books *Festival Planning Guide,* and you'll agree that a small retreat is a cake-walk in terms of planning and behind-the-scenes work.)

Still, there are few things that need to be done to help the event run smoothly. Most of what I call "admin" tasks fall into two broad categories: Budget and Communication.

Budget

Our budget is very small. Shoestring. This retreat's financial goal, though, is only to support itself. We aren't looking to make a profit, per se. In fact, as mentioned earlier in this handbook, financial accessibility has always been a big part of our ethos. Keeping this retreat within the means of Midwestern women with limited income is a priority in our planning process.

The numbers that I am sharing here are representative of our revenues and expenses, but they do not reflect the specifics of any given year.

Expenses:

Venue rental = $500

Portable toilet rental = $100/each (We get at least 4.)

Journals = $5 each

Printing (check-in forms, schedules, coloring pages, handouts) = $50

Materials/Supplies = *varies (anywhere from $0-$200)

Food = $50-$200

First Aid kit = $40

Total Expenses = $1665

Revenues:

Facilitator registrations = 10 @ $25 each = $250

Youth/Elder registrations = 5 @$40 each = $200

Regular registrations = 20 @ $60 each = $1200

Total Revenue = $1650

As you can see, the numbers are pretty tight. At most, there is usually about $200 that carries from one year to the next, which typically allows us a little wiggle room for reserving the venue, ordering another potty, or adding to our supplies. However, it is worth noting that in most years, we break even. (And occasionally, Asteria Books subsidizes the retreat by donating whatever cash is needed to make up the deficit.)

Fluctuations ~ There are always some chaos factors, as well. In some years, we have more scholarship attendees, for example, which means we bring in less from registrations. We don't do a print-run of journals every single year. And some years are very supply heavy.

Fundraising and Sponsorships ~ We've never looked into fundraising or seeking sponsorships, but these are certainly ideas that could be explored if we start noticing that we are struggling to meet our financial needs as a retreat.

First Aid, Fire, Security, Personal Care, Goddess Circle Facilitators ~ These are our "barter" roles for the event. Because we have a baseline materials cost, which includes venue rental and equipment (mainly portable toilets) rental, all of our barters are asked to contribute $25 (at the current time) for their entry to off-set costs. This is different than many other events at Midian, where many of these barters qualify for free admission. Due to our self-restricted size, though, we aren't able to provide a totally cost-free admission to anyone except 1-2 scholarship recipients each year.

Purse Warden ~ At the current time, all aspects of the budget are handled by Laurelei, as the owner of Asteria Books & Events, the parent organization for the retreat. In the future (when Laurelei is ready to retire from event-planning), we will make a plan for handing over the financial management of the Women's Goddess Retreat to an individual or a small board of directors. (More about that in "Future Planning: Succession.")

Communication

Communication leading up to the event is usually fairly simple. Our retreat community is built on a foundation of communication, which I believe makes this part of retreat planning easier on all of us.

Confirming Goddesses and Circle Facilitators ~ Sometime around January, I usually start turning my attention back to the upcoming year's retreat. For me, that involves pulling out my WGR journal to review the notes I made at the previous Closing Circle. That is the time when attendees usually let us know if they are interested in presenting, as well as which Goddesses they hear asking for inclusion.

Using intuition and divination, I listen first for the Goddesses to confirm to me that they are ready. From there, I reach out to the women who volunteered to present to see if they are still interested and available.

Sometimes women are eager to present, but they aren't sure which Goddess or what the lesson might be. In these cases, I have tended to favor volunteers with a clearer vision of what they are being called to do. In my experience, we have enjoyed the most engaging and Spirit-led Circles when both the Goddess and her Facilitator are both clear on what they will be doing.

Website and Registration Portal ~ The website for this retreat is embedded into the Asteria Books website. We use PayPal as our primary online payment option, though in recent years, we have also made Venmo and CashApp options available. At the time of this writing, we are a small operation, so I personally handle the web maintenance and collection of payments. In the coming years, this should shift to guarantee continuity of operation beyond my ability to manage it. NOTE: We close the registration portal about a month before the retreat so we can purchase journal, arrange for the potties, and buy other supplies.

Registration Confirmation ~ Once per week during the registration period. Confirmation letters should be sent to the women who have registered. These can be very simple. Something like: "We received your payment (or non-refundable deposit) for the Women's Goddess Retreat. We look forward to seeing you in October at Midian Events — 1093 Boone Hollow Rd, Springville, IN. Please watch your email in September for additional details and reminders."

Reminder Letters ~ Two to three weeks before the retreat, we send reminder letters to every registered attendee for whom we have an email address. This letter is quite long, but it includes a lot of vital information — especially for our newer attendees. A copy of the 2024 reminder letter is included at the end of this chapter.

Retreat Check-In ~ In the last couple of years, we have moved to digital check-in as attendees arrive on-site. Every person on the land, regardless of their relationship to the space or the event, is required to sign our "waiver" (Release of Liability & Hold Harmless). A copy of that is also included at the end of this chapter. We also collect some other information at check-in, including copy of photo ID to verify identity and purchase, email address along with an opt-in for our email list, and vehicle information in case we need to locate a car's owner while we are in progress. A few print copies should be available in case the digital options are not accessible.

Digital check-in can look like a printed page with QR codes for the check-in form (hosted on Google Drive) and payment options. In this scenario, women use a phone (theirs or a friend's) to check themselves in. Alternately, we might use a tablet or laptop owned by a primary organizer (or the event itself) to collect the data.

All attendees should be checked in and paid-in-full by Friday afternoon.

Journals ~ The journals we provide to attendees also act like a program, in some ways. In the past, Natalie and I printed new journals each year, which allowed us to customize the cover with a lotus mandala featuring symbols of that retreat's Goddesses, as well as including the schedule inside the largely blank book. However, we quickly realized that we were setting ourselves up for a big expense and a lot of waste. Most women aren't able to fill the entire journal with reflections from a single retreat, which meant a lot of mostly blank books.

These days, we use the WGR logo (a Nile Goddess backed by the lotus mandala) on the cover and have interior sections dedicated to retreat intentions and norms, Midian's rules, a map of the venue, and the chants we use most often.

The remaining pages are left fully blank so that women can use them to draw, make maps or charts, take notes, and record their reflections.

Retreat Facilitators should make a point to record the following information in their own journals during each Goddess Circle:

- Goddess name and Lesson(s)

- Circle Facilitator

- Activity description

- Share-time discussion prompt

Online WGR Community ~ In 2013, we created a Facebook group for attendees of the retreat. Only women who had attended the retreat were able to join, thereby reinforcing the "subrosa" expectations. In 2024, I announced that we will be officially moving that online community to Discord, as a more accessible option for the many of us who have chosen to step away from typical social media. (Discord is still a social platform, but it is considerably easier to control and curate what one sees.) In future years, as trends and platforms continue to shift, WGR should stay flexible (and vigilant) about where the community should be hosted. Privacy and mental wellness are always a top concern for us.

The group should have a cadre of moderators who can approve and remove members, as needed, as well as spark conversation and communication between retreats.

In 2020 and 2021, we also hosted a series of monthly streaming video meetings. Participation was relatively low, but this outreach did provide the ability for some of our more isolated women to stay in touch with the community.

Email List ~ Our email list is built from the opt-ins on our check-in form. This email list should never be used for spam or solicitation. It is mainly intended as a way to announce retreat registration opening and closing dates, as well as way to announce events associated with the retreat (like the new Priestex retreat, the Apotheosis retreat, or women's gatherings hosted by our retreat community).

2024 WGR Reminder Letter

PLEASE READ THIS DOCUMENT BEFORE THE RETREAT.

Midian's Women's Goddess Retreat 2024 is almost here, and we're looking forward to seeing you! Just a few reminders before you pack up and make the trip to Midian. (This is a long but vitally important message. It is NOT exactly the same as past years, so please read the whole thing.)

* Midian Festivals and Events is located at 4093 Boone Hollow Road, Springville, IN 47462. I (Laurelei) I'm the primary point of contact for this event, and I do not have cell reception at Midian -- nor do I want it. If you need to reach me, please DM Mardoll Brisingamen via Facebook Messenger, and she will get your message to me, as she is able. (It's a retreat for her, too, so please reserve all non-time-sensitive questions for Monday, when we have returned to society.)

* This women's retreat is inclusive of ALL women (cis, trans, non-binary, straight, queer, Pagan, Christian, agnostic, ALL racial and ethnic identities, etc). We are a community of women who recognize that we are stronger, healthier, and more whole because we are diverse. We explore our shared and individual womanhood so that we might better understand our own experiences and be supportive of each other.

* You will be required to show your ID at the registration table in the main pavilion when you arrive. It is also wise to have proof of registration in case there is an error in our records. (Your PayPal receipt or the email confirmation you received both work for this purpose. You can download them to a mobile device instead of printing, if you prefer.) If you don't have your ID, you WILL be refused admission.

* Check-In is digital this year. We'll have QR codes for both registration and also PayPal. (You can also pay any fees you owe in cash.) We'll also have some printed copies of the registration form in case anyone struggles with the digital version.

* All attendees are HIGHLY encouraged to arrive and be present for the opening circle, which begins at 12pm on Friday, October 4, and to attend all circles throughout the weekend. Our opening is designed to help us form the community of women, as it will be for the weekend, and the closing is intended to give us all closure before reintegrating into the world. While we understand if your travel needs dictate a late arrival or early departure, please understand that the experience will be more challenging for you, as well as for us, if you are unable to attend the opening. If this is your situation, it is even more crucial that you attend the other circles and inundate yourself within the culture and climate of the retreat as much as possible.

* You may arrive as early as 4pm on Thursday evening to set up camp and get acclimated to the space. The gates will be open 4-9pm Thursday evening and will reopen at 9am on Friday morning. They will be closed for privacy and protection (though not locked) starting at 12pm on Friday (the beginning of our opening circle). If you arrive after the gates are closed, please WALK back to the pavilion (a short walk along Midian's only road) to sign in and join the circle in progress. You will then be able to open the gate for yourself to drive your vehicle into the camping space to set up during the break. If you are being dropped off by a male family member or friend, please understand that he will need to stay outside the gate once the retreat has actually begun. This is a clothing optional event (for women 18+), and some of our attendees only feel safe enough to explore this freedom because we have offered

them a woman-only space. (If he is dropping you off during a circle and you need to unpack, you can use a wheelbarrow or wagon to cart your gear back to your campsite. We very much encourage early arrival to get set up.)

* Most of your questions can be answered at our FAQ page:

http://www.asteriabooks.com/retreat/info.html

*This event features a pitch-in dinner on Friday night. We encourage you to join other retreat attendees in this communal meal. (There will not be a kitchen vendor available at any time this weekend.) You should plan to bring enough of your contribution to share with 4-6 people. (If we all bring a little to share, we'll truly see a great abundance.) If you have food allergies, be sure to bring something you know is safe for you. WARNING: ONE OF OUR REGULAR ATTENDEES HAS AN AIRBORNE CINNAMON ALLERGY. DO NOT BRING ANYTHING THAT CONTAINS CINNAMON. If you bring something that needs to be warm, please bring a hot plate, crock pot, or other warming tray. (We have electricity!) We also encourage bringing a washable plate, cup, bowl, and utensils to cut down on paper waste. We will have a wash station set up to make clean-up a little easier. (We will provide some paper plates/bowls, wooden disposable utensils, etc). (This list is offered as a *guideline.* Feel free to bring your specialty/favorite, even if it isn't what is "assigned.")

Aries - Entree

Taurus - Vegetable

Gemini - Fruit

Cancer - Pasta

Leo - Bread

Virgo - Salad

Libra - Beverage

Scorpio - Dessert

Sagittarius - Appetizer/finger food

Capricorn - Soup/Stew

Aquarius - Dip/Chips

Pisces - Side Dish

* NEW in 2024 -- We're going to offer some communal food options for Saturday and Sunday, as well. The retreat will provide chili and corn-bread on Saturday (dinner); and we'll provide chicken noodles, mashed potatoes, and rolls on Sunday (lunch). We will gladly accept donations of fixin's, side dishes, chips, desserts, or money from anyone who wants to support this. (You are not required to bring/donate anything to have some of this food. I'm just feeling compelled to make sure there is plen-ty of warm food on hand. (Note: the chili will have ground beef and sausage. It will NOT have cinnamon.) Also: Bringing your own bowl and spoon could be a good plan. (Or a mug! See below.)

* Bring your Mug! There will be wassail, hot coffee, and hot water avail-able all weekend. Bring your own mug to help us cut down on paper trash.

* This event no longer has a Kitchen Goddess. Please plan for your own food needs throughout the weekend (which can include the chili and chicken noodles mentioned above). Pro Tip: Reduce your heat, effort, and stress this weekend by bringing foods that can be eaten cold/room temp. (Several of us keep a cooler and a "dry foods box" with us at/

near the Pavilion the whole weekend. Everyone is welcome to do the same!)

* If you registered for a woman other than yourself, it is unlikely that her email address is in our registration logs -- which means she isn't receiving this message. Please forward this message to the other members of your party and print a copy of your receipt/confirmation for them, particularly if you will be arriving separately.

* If you reserved your admission with the non-refundable Save-My-Spot, you will owe the remaining amount (payable by PayPal or cash, preferably in the exact amount to cut down on our limited ability to make change during a circle in progress) when you arrive. That'll either be $35 (standard) or $15 (if you are an elder/youth).

* If you attended the retreat in the last couple of years and you still have your WGR journal with a usable amount of pages, you are encouraged to bring it with you for use this year. If you want/need a new journal (or if this is your first year), we will happily provide one.

* Queening Rite this year. I think we have 5 Queens ready to be crowned this year. Any of our attendees who feels moved to don the mantle of the Queen is welcomed to take part. Others are welcomed to bring gifts for these Queens -- if it is your will to do so. And women who have been previously crowned are encouraged to bring and wear their crowns, rings, and sashes.

* Crossing Rite this year. We are honoring the crossing of two of our sisters -- Becca and Bonnie. These women donned the mantle of Elder/

Crone with us in 2010, and they have both gone to join the Ancestors as of this spring. You are encouraged to bring offerings for one or both of these remarkable women, if you are moved. (Any offerings that are left in our care will be transported to the Ancestor Shrine after the Closing Circle on Sunday.)

* "Unseen Sisters" Seat. Starting in 2024, we will place a seat in our Circle for the Sisters who are unable to join us in the flesh. They may have crossed, moved, or simply be unable to be present due to work and life circumstances. If you have pictures, mementos, or items you would like to place on the "Unseen Sisters" Chair, please feel encouraged to bring them.

* Parking is permitted inside our gates, and you may camp in your vehicle, if you desire. Please use good judgment in choosing your campsite in this case, as towing fees can be quite costly. Vehicles should not block any roadways at any time.

* Be prepared for any type of weather -- HOT, cold, wet or dry. Our camping spots are not reserved. Portable shade (umbrella/parasol) is always a GREAT idea, as is a portable fan. And since we have migrated to an October weekend, you might be wise to include some extra "hot stuff" for the nights -- hand warmers, hot water bottles, extra blankets, thermals/long-janes. =)

* We encourage you to perform your own magick and ceremonies during our breaks, and there are several sites on the grounds that may inspire your magick! (Ancestors' Shrine, Freya's Shrine, Aphrodite's Shrine, Hekate's Shrine, Artemis's Shrine, and Bardic Circle are just a FEW of the points of interest.)

* We operate "subrosa" during the entirety of the retreat. What is said "under the sign of the rose" is said in confidence. Women at the retreat often share very painful truths, very private confessions, and very sensitive realities. While you are at full liberty to share your own revelations or to talk about the cool activities we did in a general way, it is a grievous betrayal of trust to tell another woman's story or to share the role she played in our circle.

* Group Altar – As is our tradition, we will establish a group altar in the center of our meeting space. Please bring any Goddess-related objects that you would like to contribute to this space for the weekend. Whatever you bring is still yours to keep, of course. Consider bringing statues, potted or dried herbs, candles, incense, stones, or other symbols to create sacred space, honor the Goddesses of the retreat, the Goddesses who walk with you wherever you go, or even represent that which is divine within you. (Our Goddesses this year are Athena, Nike, Durga, Brighid, Echo, and the Great Goddess.) You can also bring things to decorate the pavilion, if you like -- Goddess flags, tapestries, flower garlands, etc. (Some of Psyche's butterflies are still on our posts from a previous retreat.) Just bring the necessary items for hanging them, as well -- and remember that you are responsible for removing them before you leave.

* We no longer have recycling bins for glass, plastic bottles, paper, and aluminum. Attendees are encouraged to bring as little as possible that will turn into landfill trash. Otherwise, as in past years, you pack out your trash and take it home for disposal. We will provide trashbags, if you need them. PRO TIP: REMOVE PACKAGING FROM NEW ITEMS BEFORE YOU PACK YOUR GEAR TO REDUCE WASTE AT CAMP.

* Midian HQ ("ask Laurelei"), First Aid, and Security will be present in the pavilion at the many circles all weekend long. If a problem arises in the night, Laurelei and Holly will be camping in "Cabin Black" out in the parking lot.

* We observe quiet hours from midnight to 8 am. It is the expectation that all women at the retreat will be present for all the circles, unless otherwise attending to their needs and their own intention for the retreat (eg, the Sacred Nap). You're welcome to stay up past midnight, of course; just keep it quiet.

* Smoking in Circle – As a courtesy to those who may be allergic or otherwise physically troubled by smoke, please do your best to position yourself upwind and on the outer edges of the circle if you choose to smoke during circle-time. We will attempt to provide sufficient breaks between circles, as well. At no time (including breaks), will smoking be permitted under the pavilion.

* Holding the Container -- There are many aspects (some subtle, some obvious) to holding the space for each other throughout the retreat that enable us to do the deep, transformative work that allows us to grow, flourish, and bond the way that way do each year. Be mindful of the space and the sanctity of the Circle, especially when another woman has the Rattle. If you need to step away to process something with a trusted sister, take it out of earshot of the Circle. If you need a break from an intense moment, take it -- but not at the expense of the work happening for another woman/group. Let her/them have their process.

* Vending is free to all women at the retreat. Bring a table to set up in the Admin Building. (The building will be locked at night when Laurelei

goes to bed.) If you bring things to sell, mark each item with your name and the price, and bring a box/jar/can of some sort to collect payment when you might not be at the table. You can also sell items/services from your campsite or set up a booth, if that pleases you.

* Retreat Library. Back again after a 14-year break! Laurelei is bringing a bunch of Goddess, retreat, and women-care related titles to act as a lending library for anyone who wants to read a little as part of her self-care at the retreat. There will be a sign-out sheet, and all books must be returned before set-up for the Circle of the Great Goddess begins on Sunday morning. If you have some books you would like to share for the weekend, make sure your name is printed in the inside cover and bring them out. (NOTE: We did this in 2009 and 2010, but a couple of pricey/rare books were not returned, which bummed us out and kinda hurt our feelings. I'm feeling brave to try this again, though, given the remarkable group of women who join us year after year.)

* Wisdom Tent. We're going to set up a little quiet corner for women who want to be "alone, but maybe also together" in quiet reflection during our breaks. The retreat will provide the ez-up canopy and maybe some fabric to drape around it. If anyone else wants to contribute cushions, little tables, candles, or anything they think might make the place cozy and comfy for the weekend, thank you! Like other items, you'll want to collect these before leaving on Sunday.

* Have fun and take care of yourself. Stay hydrated and sun-sheltered. Ice cold water is available from our well 24/7, so carry a reusable water bottle to refill as needed.

We look forward to seeing you there.

Asteria Projects Team

(Laurelei & friends -- both visible and invisible)

WOMEN'S GODDESS RETREAT 1. INFORMED CONSENT, RELEASE OF LIABILITY AND INDEMNITY AGREEMENT2. FESTIVAL RULES AGREEMENT

PLEASE READ CAREFULLY

1.) I am aware that participation in the Women's Goddess Retreat involves many risks, dangers, and hazards including, but not limited to: changing weather conditions; risk of heat stroke; exposed rock, earth, and other natural objects; trees, tree wells, tree stumps, forest dead fall; steep and uneven terrain; streams, creeks; bonfires, burns, sunburn; allergies; wild animals; tone deaf singing, possible negligence of other campers, and possible negligence on the part of Asteria Projects and/or Midian, LLP or its officers, directors, and members.

I AM AWARE OF THE RISKS, DANGERS, AND HAZARDS ASSOCIATED WITH PRIMITIVE CAMPING AND WITH THIS PARTICULAR EVENT, AND I FREELY ACCEPT AND FULLY ASSUME ALL LEGAL AND PHYSICAL RISKS, DANGERS, AND HAZARDS AND THE POSSIBILITY OF PERSONAL INJURY, DEATH, PROPERTY DAMAGE OR LOSS RESULTING THEREFROM ON BEHALF OF MYSELF AND THOSE IN MY CHARGE.

I declare that my physical condition, to the best of my knowledge, is adequate to participate safely in primitive camping and that no physician or other qualified individual has advised me against participating in such trips.

I authorize Asteria Projects and/or Midian, LLP to secure such medical and/or other advice and services as it, in its sole discretion, may deem necessary for my health and safety should it be necessary in an emergency.

In consideration of participating in the Women's Goddess Retreat at Midian, I agree to be financially responsible for all costs and expenses which may be incurred with respect to rescues, travel, medical attention or other services provided on behalf of myself and agree to reimburse Asteria Books or any third party for all costs of these services.

2.) I agree to abide by the rules of Midian and Asteria Projects (stated below) and understand that failure to comply with these rules may result in being removed from this festival. I understand that a copy of these rules is provided with my personal festival entrance kit and is accessible at both the WGR-HQ station.

RULES

1. This retreat obeys all local and state ordinances and laws. All firearms, all illegal drugs, or any alcoholic beverages not intended for personal consumption are not permitted.

2. Pets, other than registered service animals, are not permitted. Service animals must be leashed and well-behaved at all times. The human is responsible for cleaning up all messes made by their animal.

4. Vehicle camping is permitted. Please make sure your vehicle is clear of any roadways. Vehicle owner/driver assumes all liability and financial responsibility associated with their vehicle while on the Midian grounds. This includes damage to/by vehicle, as well as towing and/or repairs, if needed.

5. No filming (camcorders, video equipment, phone cameras) is allowed during the retreat. Photography is permitted only if prior permission is requested of anyone whose photo you may be taking. This includes individuals in the background area of your shot. Permission to photograph does not imply permission to post photos publicly, which express permission must also be granted. Failure to comply with these rules may result in removal from the festival and/or a ban from future events.

6. Women's Goddess Retreat is a clothing-optional event (away from roads and creek, which are public spaces). Please remember that nudity is not an invitation to invasion of personal space. Affirmative, on-going consent is required at all times, and security staff is available to assist with violations of privacy and personal sovereignty.

7. Keep your camp area cleared of trash and clutter. No cigarette butts or other debris are to be tossed on any part of the grounds. Burn paper waste at your own campsite. Pack out your trash and gear. Any person who leaves debris at their campsite, vending area, or other location may be fined up to $250 for clean-up and/or banned from attending future events, at the sole discretion of the event owner.

8. Glass bottles/containers will not be allowed around the main fire. Please decant your beverages into a plastic or metal container.

9. This retreat respects all races, genders, sexual orientations, spiritual paths, and other protected identifiers. Exhibitions of bigotry and intolerance WILL get you removed from this festival -- at the sole discretion of the retreat director.

10. No climbing on any rocks or walls, and no traversing the Badlands. These areas are strictly prohibited, for the safety of all.

11. There are no refunds given for the retreat at this time for any reason, including removal from the event by Staff.

I have read, understood, and accept the above consents and agreements.

Notes

Notes

Future Planning

This retreat is a blessing and a boon in the lives of so many! I remember Natalie telling me in the early years of the retreat that she had originally envisioned it as a one-time event. A retreat experience was needed for the women of Our Haven Nature Sanctuary, the first home of WGR. Hearing the call, she laid the groundwork.

Not only was that first event in 2009 wildly successful in its own right, but it laid the foundation for a community that continues to thrive and grow. What's more, it holds the promise of vibrancy and impact well beyond the ability of its current stewards to carry forward this work. In short, I am hopeful that this event will outlive me and the current cadre of Facilitators.

This book, then, is a "love offering" to my daughter and all the daughters who will carry these traditions forward.

What Can Change and What Remains Constant

As I contemplate the legacy of this event, I find it important to contemplate the ways that it might evolve when the current generation of stewards slow down and step aside.

It is hard to envision the specifics of those potential changes. Technology, economy, political climate, venue, and changes in personal freedoms could all have impacts, for good or ill.

Perhaps it is more vital that we define those things that should be kept at the heart of this work. For that, I refer you back to the essays and musings included in the chapter titled "Culture and History of Our Retreat." The reflections there reflect the core values of this event, which we've collectively defined and refined over the last 15 or so years. Those values are the beating heart of this work, and the structure (discussed in the chapter that follows those reflections) provides the container.

Think deeply about changes as they present themselves. Our driving question, ALWAYS, remains:

"Does this support my/our retreat intention?"

A Few Ideas

We have a few ideas already in the works that probably need some project leaders and teams to handle.

* **Anthology of essays and reflections** — I would love to see a book or series of books that share specific lessons, activities, and insights gained from our Goddess Circles and Rites of Passage. My vision for this is to curate essays and reflections from a variety of attendees in order to showcase the myriad voices and perspectives represented by our community. Look for a submission form soon on the retreat website!

* **Coloring books** — This one is already under way! I've started drawing coloring pages and compiling them into coloring books. 2009 and 2024 are ready now on Amazon. 2010 and 2025, at least, will be finished before the 2025 retreat.

* **Red Tents** — We have erected a Red Tent at a couple of our retreats, but this almost certainly needs a team of its own. Traditionally, the Red Tent is a place where menstruating women can go to rest, meditate, and commune with other women experiencing their moon blood. As our retreat, this tends to be a quiet space open to any women (bleeding or not) who is looking for companionable quietness. It is a place to meditate and be still without disappearing into the isolation of a personal campsite.

* **On-Site Library** — Natalie and I brought tubs full of books to the first two retreats, and I revived the tradition in 2024. It is a handful, though, for one of the primary Facilitators to manage the packing and tracking

of the books. We need our own Hypatia of Alexandria to lead this effort!

* **Community Kitchen or Group Meal Coordination** — For a number of reasons, our venue no longer has a working kitchen on-site. In 2024, we started a somewhat new tradition of offering communal meal options for Saturday's dinner and Sunday's lunch. This could be expanded a bit so that the workload is shared and women are able to contribute to the care and feeding of the group.

The following ideas speak to an ethos held sacred by me, and that is the idea of "ever-widening circles of love and trust." Natalie and I always hoped this retreat's impact would grow and spread, and it has already achieved that goal. There are women's retreats patterned on this one happening in several different parts of the United States. In keeping with the inspiration we draw from ideas like the "Millionth Circle," I want to encourage this sort of outreach. We change the world by changing ourselves, and we change ourselves through circles of love and trust, like the ones we form together every autumn at Midian.

* **Monthly Online Gatherings** — These take a core of people dedicated to both facilitating and participating in order to be successful. There is room here for several women to step into service, if interested.

* **Semi-Annual Retreats** (spring and fall) — Currently, the Women's Goddess Retreat gathers in the autumn each year. We have discussed

wanting to start a vernal retreat, as well.

* **Priestex Retreat** (winter/summer?) — We've talked for years about hosting a retreat specifically for those who have been called into service by a Godd-friend. This might be women and gender non-conforming folx who are called to serve a female Goddess, male God, or non-binary Godd, but could also include men who are called into services of a Goddess or Godd. The first of these was planned for July 2025 at Driftwood Tiny Retreats — but a flood told us "Not Yet!" This is still something the community wants and needs, and I leave it to you, my Sisters, to see it through.

* **Apotheosis Retreat** — In 2026, Laurelei intends to launch this gender-inclusive retreat for personal transformation. It will operate using the same structure and values as our Women's Goddess Retreat, but it will be open to all adult members of our local community, without consideration of gender. Additionally, it will explore lessons and stories of Deities of all genders.

Succession

I'm in my Queen Years right now, and I think my Wise Woman years are still some distance ahead of me. I'm not sure when to expect their arrival, and I look forward to that phase in my life, when it comes. For now, though, I'm young at 50 and still have so much to do! So many ideas and adventures — with and for this retreat community — are still ahead of me!

That being said, I'm grateful to know this retreat will continue even when I'm ready to take a different role — that of elder and Wise Woman in our Circle of women. We have many leaders already, and I see a crop of young leaders emerging. Daughters and nieces who have undergone Menarche and Womaning rituals with us as tweens and teens. Young women who are now starting their own families and beginning to bring their own life's work into the world.

This handbook is the first (and probably biggest) step in our "succession planning." With it, you know what I know about leading this retreat.

I love you, Sister — whoever and wherever you are.

Now go! Bring the women together. Sit them in a Circle, and share stories of the Goddesses. Share the stories of ourselves.

Notes

Notes

www.ingramcontent.com/pod-product-compliance
Lightning Source LLC
LaVergne TN
LVHW051640080426
835511LV00016B/2414